CW01655331

WATERCOLOR NATURE

A Step-By-Step Guide

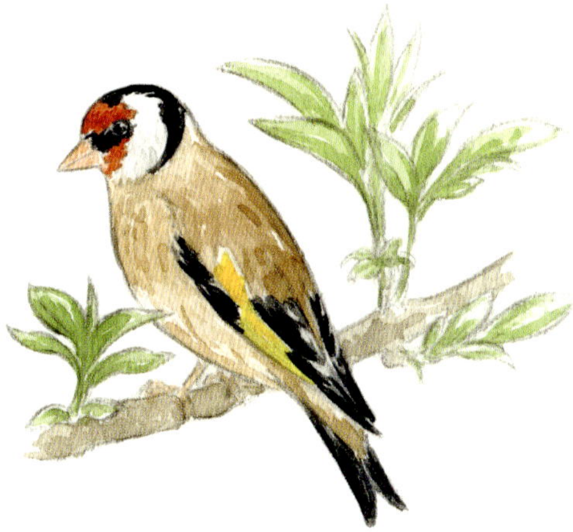

BY AMANDINE LABARRE

PETER PAUPER PRESS, INC.
White Plains, New York

For Nym

PETER PAUPER PRESS
Fine Books and Gifts Since 1928

Our Company

In 1928, at the age of twenty-two, Peter Beilenson began printing books on a small press in the basement of his parents' home in Larchmont, New York. Peter—and later, his wife, Edna—sought to create fine books that sold at "prices even a pauper could afford."

Today, still family owned and operated, Peter Pauper Press continues to honor our founders' legacy—and our customers' expectations—of beauty, quality, and value.

Written and illustrated by Amandine Labarre

English translation by Vesna Neskow, © 2017 Peter Pauper Press, Inc.

Library of Congress Cataloging-in-Publication Data

Names: Labarre, Amandine, 1980- author, illustrator. | Neskow, Vesna, translator.
Title: Watercolor nature : a step-by-step guide */ by Amandine Labarre.*
Other titles: Aquarelle. *English*
Description: White Plains, New York : Peter Pauper Press, Inc., 2017. |
"Originally published in French as Aquarelle: Une initiation pas a pas, *ISBN 978-2-2151-5029-9, Fleurus Editions, © 2012."*
Identifiers: LCCN 2016041763 | ISBN 9781441322722 (pbk.: alk. paper)
Subjects: LCSH: Watercolor painting – Technique. | Nature in art.
Classification: LCC ND2420 .L2813 2017 | DDC 704.9/43--dc23 LC record available at https://lccn.loc gov/2016041763

Copyright © 2017
Peter Pauper Press, Inc.
202 Mamaroneck Avenue
White Plains, NY 10601 USA
ISBN 978-1-4413-2272-2
Printed in China
7 6 5 4 3 2 1
Visit us at www.peterpauper.com

WATERCOLOR NATURE

A Step-By-Step Guide

By AMANDINE LABARRE

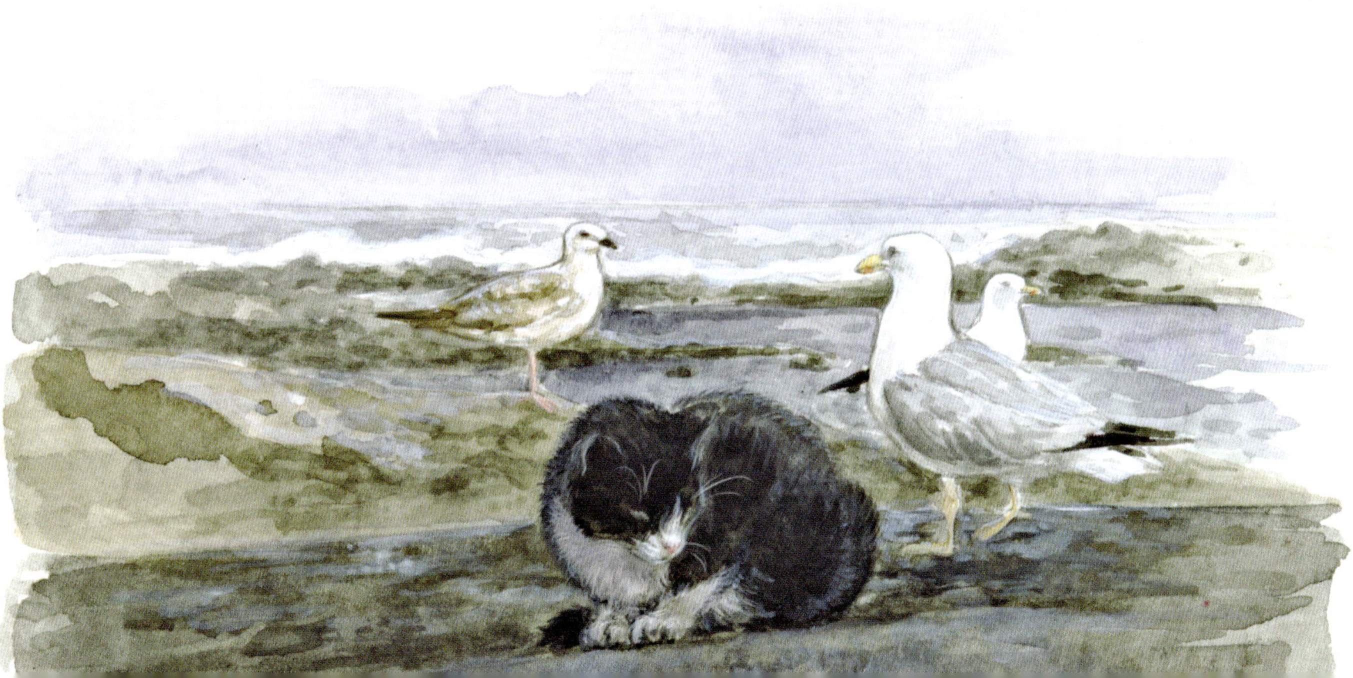

Getting Started 7

Watercolor 8

Paint Colors 9

Brushes 10

Other Supplies 10

Paper 12

Step-by-Step Painting 14

Basic Techniques 15

Basic Exercises 16

Plein Air Painting 18

In Fields and Woods 20

Crocus 22

Bulbs 25

Bramble Flowers 26

Wildflowers 28

Mistletoe 29

Sweet Pea 30

Leaves and Berries 32

Redcurrant 34

Buds and Flowers 37

Tree and Mistletoe 38

Chestnut Leaf 40

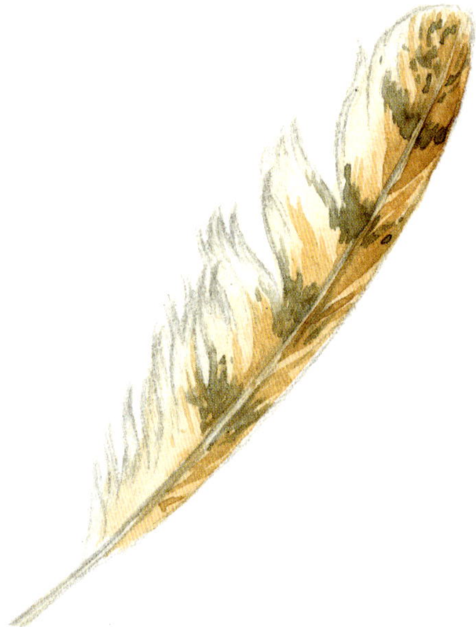

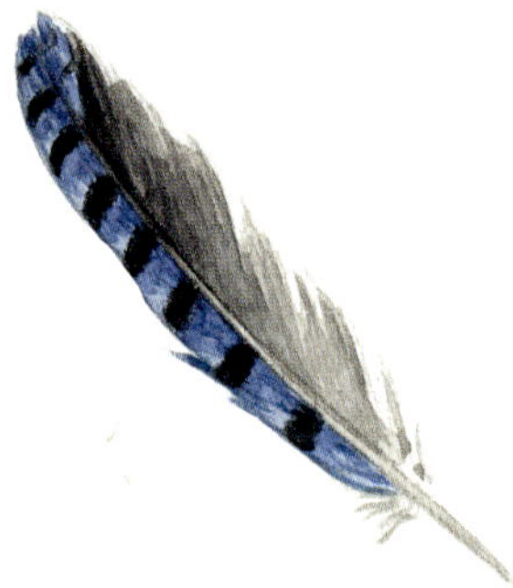

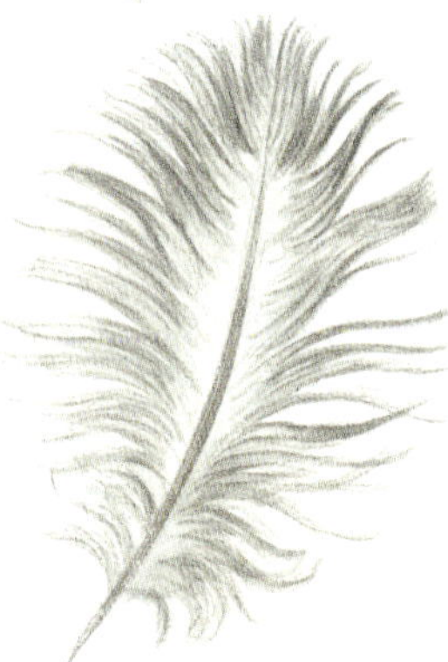

TABLE OF CONTENTS

Encounters around the Corner 42

White Cat 44
Cats 46
Red Squirrel on a Stump 47
Mare and Foal 48
Horse against a Stormy Sky 50
Swallow 52
European Goldfinch 53
Nuthatch 54
Small Animals 55
Garden Blue Tit 56
Singing Birds 59

At the Water's Edge... and Beyond 60

Nesting Seagull 62
Aquatic Birds 65
Small Sanderling 66
Bird Studies 67
Grebes 68
Hills and Sea 70
Icy Mountain 72
Snowdrop 76

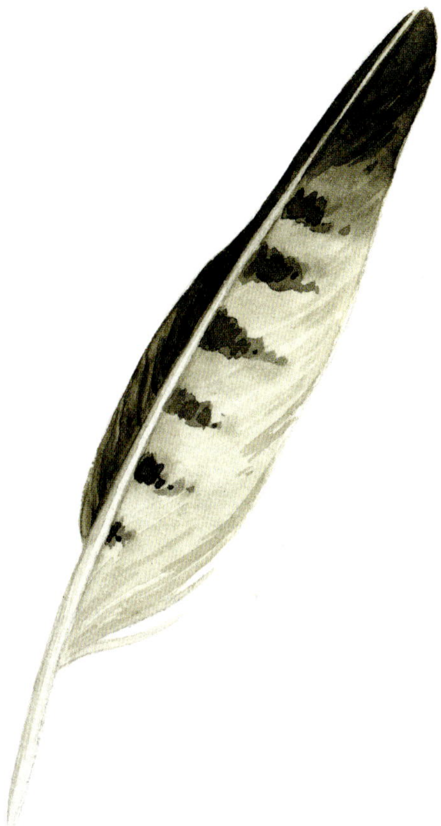

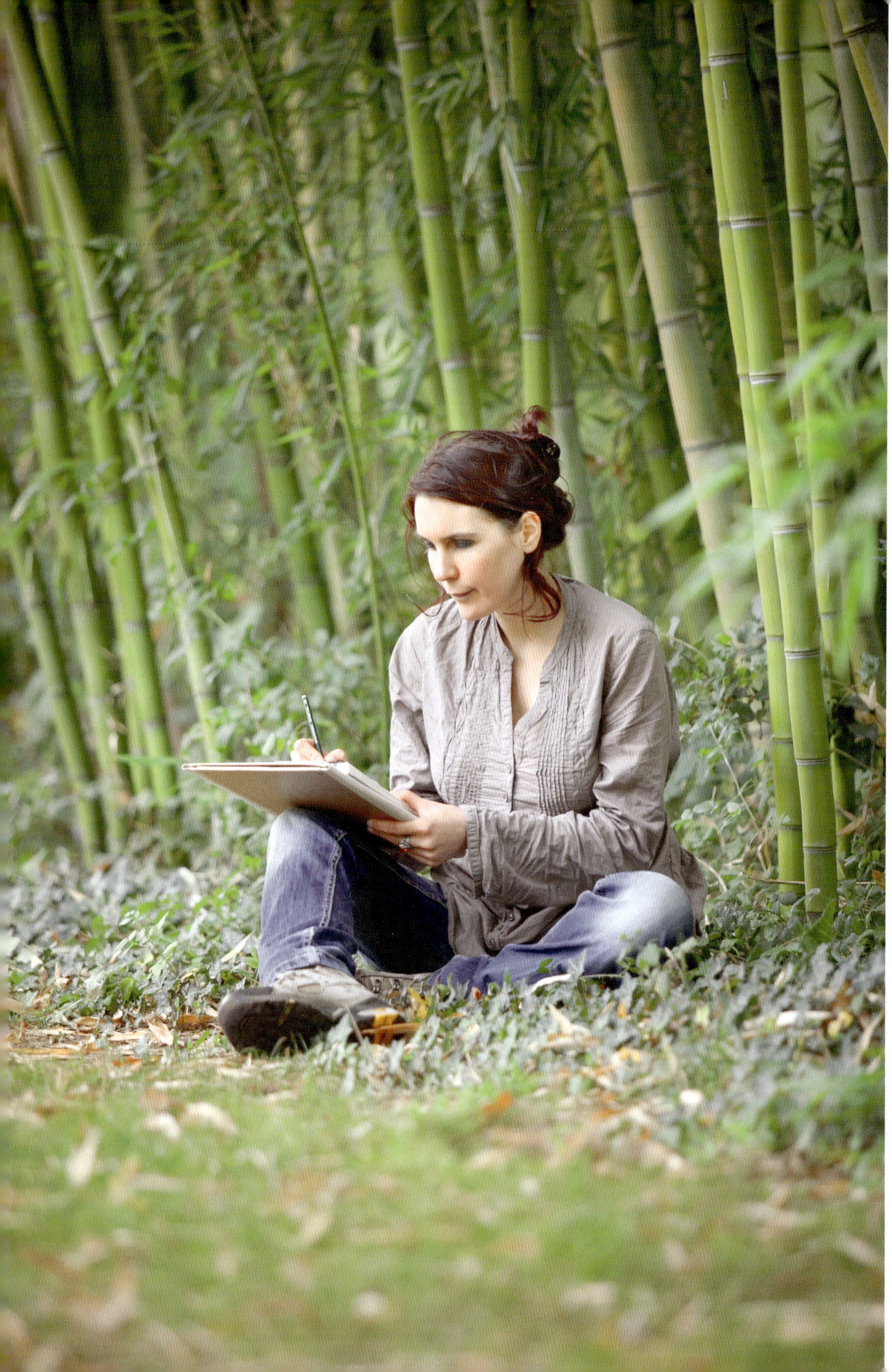

GETTING STARTED

Watercolor is a water-soluble paint with transparent colors. It has been popular with artists for centuries, especially because the easily portable materials allow painters to work anywhere. Though it is beginner-friendly, watercolor is by no means limited to beginning painters. Its rapid drying allows one to complete a work in one session—called *alla prima* in Italian. Before beginning, practice diluting and layering colors. Then observe how watercolors behave depending on how wet or dry your paper and brush are; learn to keep sections of the paper white; develop your skills following the advice of artists... and start painting the world around you!

WATERCOLOR

Watercolor comes in tubes and pans. The latter make it easier to use only as much paint as you need. In addition, watercolor pans are dry, making them more practical for transport and painting outdoors.

Paint is often marketed as "student grade" or "artist grade." Choose watercolors labeled "artist grade" or "extra fine." Richer in pigmentation, these colors are more intense and brilliant.

There are watercolor sets that include a plastic palette, but it's easier to mix colors in a separate, sturdier palette. The best palettes are made of white enameled metal or white porcelain. Large, deep wells allow you to mix colors in larger quantities.

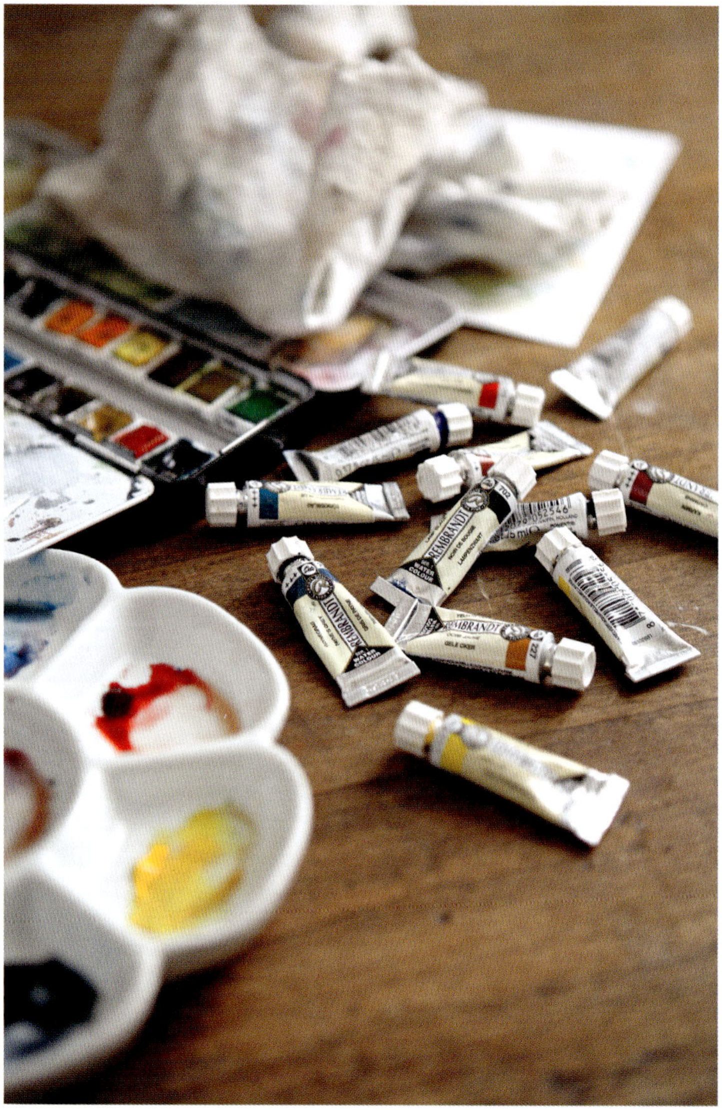

PAINT COLORS

Note: If a painting calls for a color you don't have, mix an approximation of the color or simply substitute the nearest match in your paint box. You won't match the tones shown exactly, but can almost always get close enough to follow along using the paints in any standard set of watercolors.

To start off, limit yourself to about a dozen colors. I recommend the following:

Blues: Ultramarine Blue, Cobalt Blue, Payne's Gray
Yellows: Cadmium Yellow Lemon, Yellow Ochre
Reds: Cadmium Red Deep and Light, Alizarin Crimson
Browns: Burnt Sienna, Sepia
Greens: Sap Green, Emerald Green

Later, you will gradually expand your palette according to your taste. Below are all the colors used to create the watercolors described in this book. A large range helps in avoiding elaborate blends, which can result in a dull and faded color.

Paint colors often have odd names. Why "Prussian Blue" instead of "dark blue," and "Cadmium Yellow" instead of "bright yellow"? The answer: These standard names refer to specific pigments or combinations of pigments. When you buy Cadmium Yellow (provided it's the genuine pigment and not an imitation "hue"), you know that the paint will be an intense, warm, moderately opaque yellow. You don't always have to invest in authentic pigments, especially when you're just starting out. But standard color names are useful points of reference regardless.

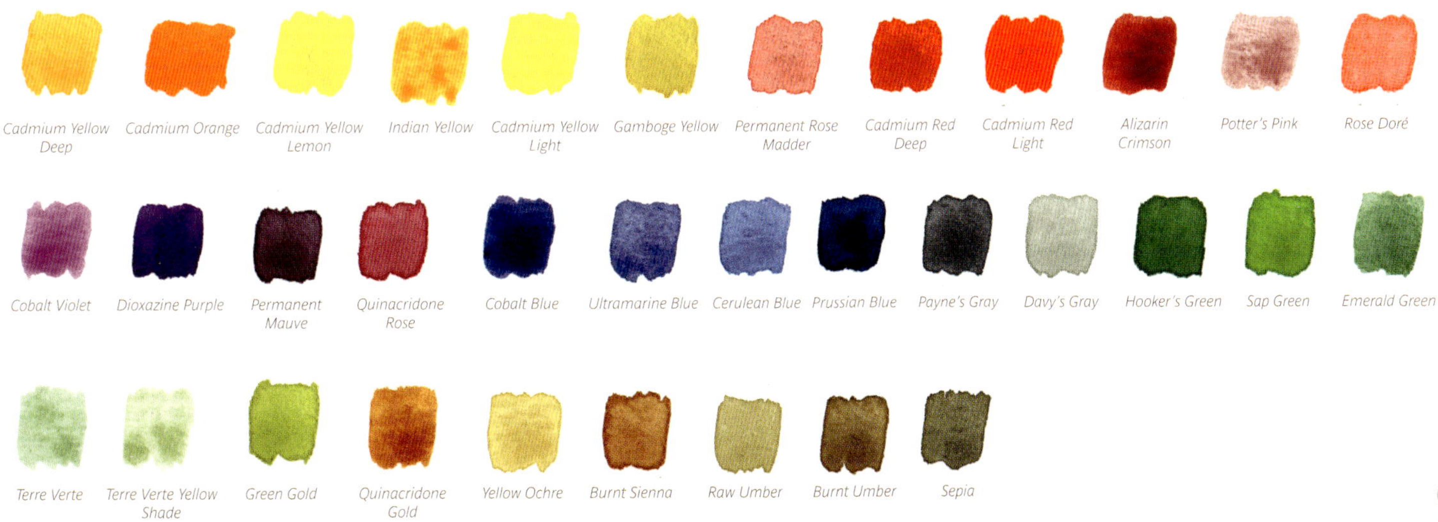

BRUSHES

Brushes with natural bristles, traditionally used for watercolor, are the most expensive but of the highest quality. You do not need a large assortment of brushes in the beginning. So choose four or five good brushes, in sable or Russian squirrel, or synthetic brushes made specifically for watercolor. There are many synthetic brushes of excellent quality for artists who would prefer not to use animal hair. A brush is characterized by the width of its tuft (corresponding to a number) as well as its shape. Each has its own function.

The **wash brush**, with a round tip, is used to apply washes on large surfaces and to "sponge up" excess water.

The **round brush**, with a pointed tip, allows you to both color and draw.

The **slender-tipped round brush** is the most precise of the three. It is used to paint the most delicate details.

After each use, wash your brushes with warm water, then make sure they are dry before laying them flat, protected from dust, or in a cup with the brush tips pointing upward. Never leave them to soak, or else the bristles may become irreparably misshapen.

OTHER SUPPLIES

Make sure you have a 2B pencil, which is soft enough for sketching, and a kneaded eraser, which will not damage the paper. Also have two containers filled with water, to rinse your brushes between colors, and a cloth to dry them.

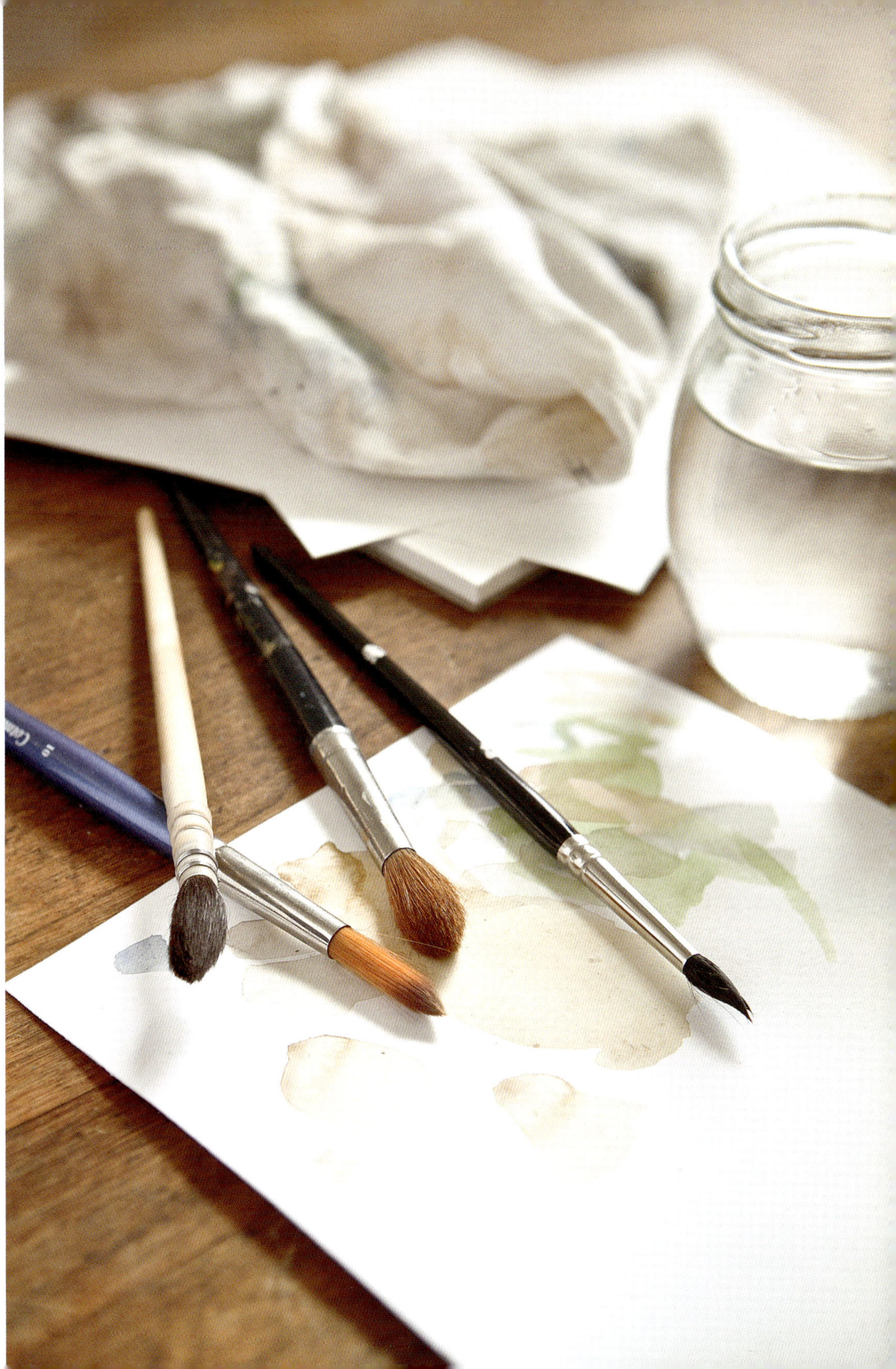

PAPER

Various types of paper are especially well suited to watercolor, most with 100% cotton or a wood filler base. The various thicknesses are noted by weight in grams per square meter. The 300 g/m^2 (or 300 gsm) weight, in the middle of the range, is most commonly used. Lighter-weight paper than 300 gsm should be stretched on a drawing board to avoid wrinkling. Heavier paper is more absorbent and will hold its form without stretching.

There are three main types of surfaces: fine grain or smooth, medium grain, and rough grain or torchon grain. Painting on smooth paper is easier for a beginner. Coarser paper allows for more interesting effects but is not well suited to creating delicate details.

Blocks of paper are perfect for painting outdoors; the taut paper will not buckle when wet. Spiral pads are best used for sketches and rapid studies.

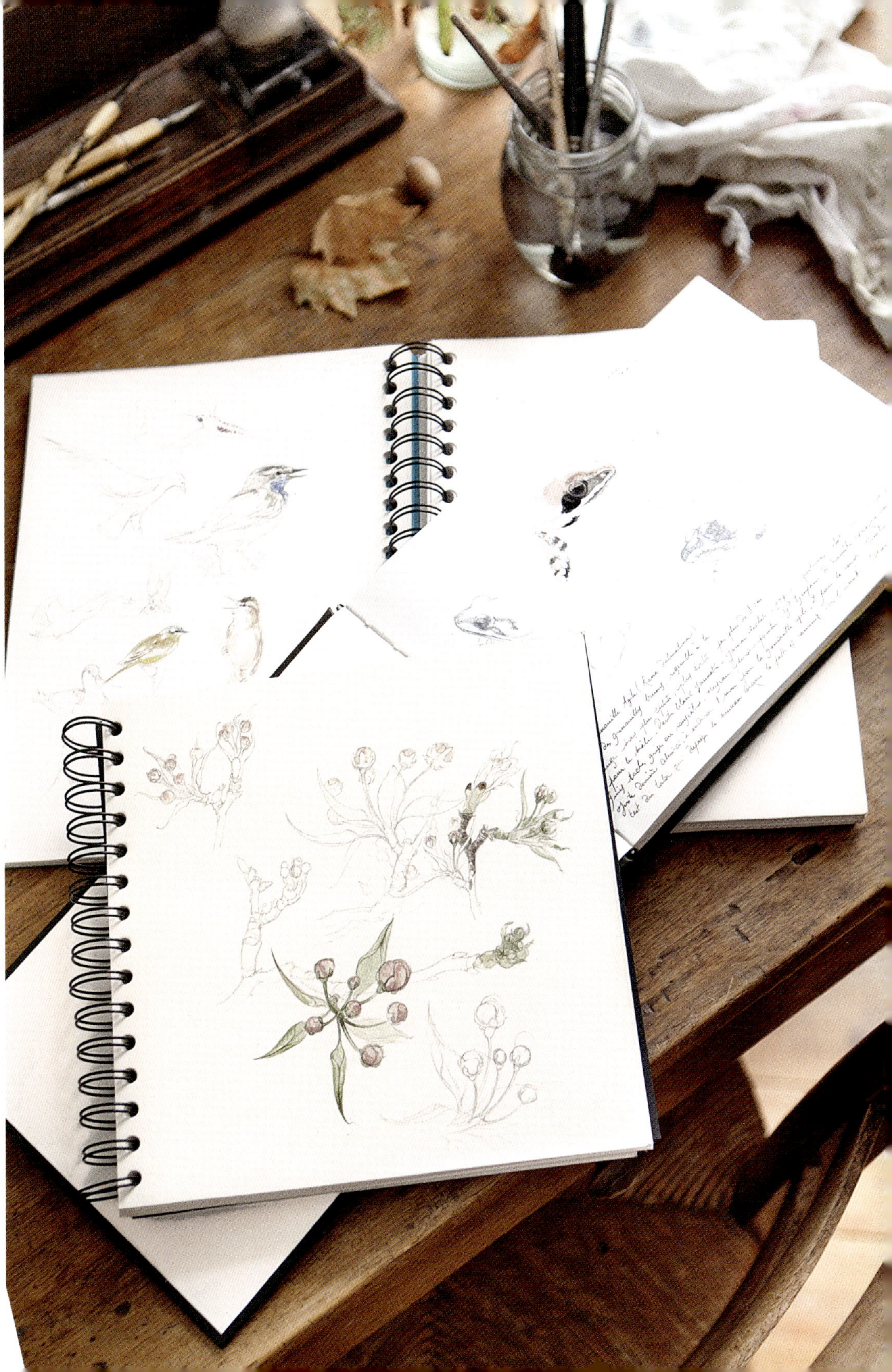

STEP-BY-STEP PAINTING

Start by sketching your subject with a soft, well-sharpened pencil. Since watercolor is translucent, the pencil lines will be visible beneath the color. Therefore, draw lightly. It isn't necessary to draw every detail; your work will become freer and more powerful if you envision watercolor not as a coloring technique but as a different sort of art altogether.

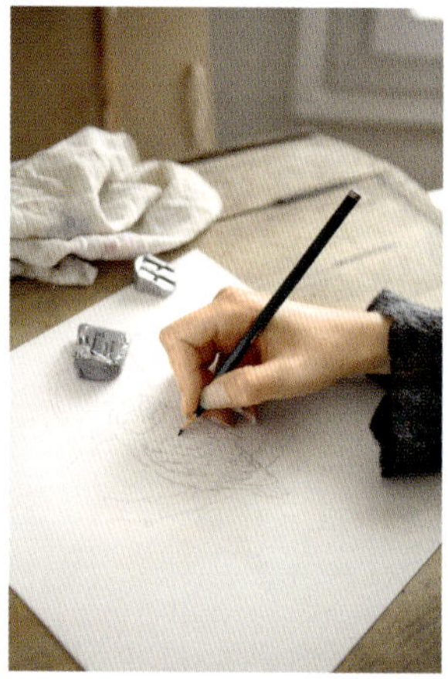

Apply the color in successive washes (a bit of color mixed with water). This will render the colors progressively denser and darker, and balance the highlights. Always go from lighter to darker, and develop the painting as a whole, rather than finishing one color or area after another. The lightest color is the white of the paper. Consider from the beginning which areas you will leave untouched or lightly painted, and reserve the white of the paper in certain areas of the drawing to maintain luminosity.

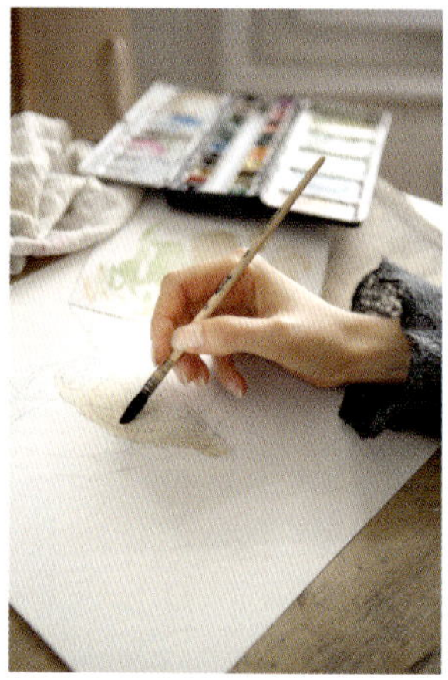

Once the light and shadow are balanced, add the details with a fine brush.

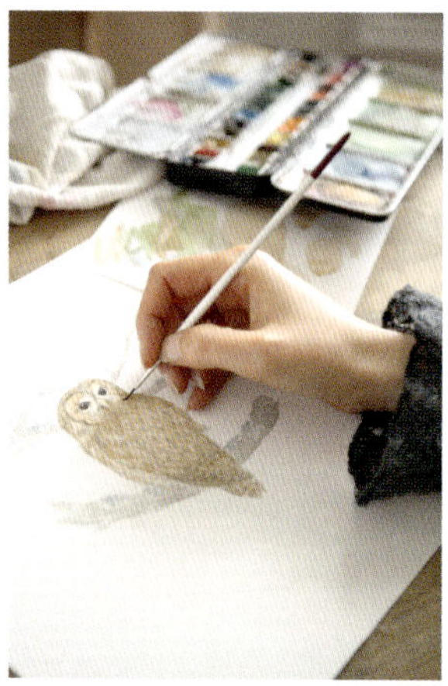

BASIC TECHNIQUES

There are two basic techniques in watercolor that offer very different effects: wet-on-wet and wet-on-dry.

Wet-on-Wet

This technique allows you to create gradations of color and soft backgrounds. Here, I have wet the paper by brushing water within the contours of the subject. Then I successively layered Yellow Ochre and Indian Yellow on the wet area: the two colors have partially merged. On this still moist surface, I next applied touches of Burnt Sienna and Cadmium Red Light. The color becomes more or less diffuse depending on how wet the paper is. While the paint is still wet, you can also remove excess moisture by "sponging" it up with a Q-tip or a dry brush.

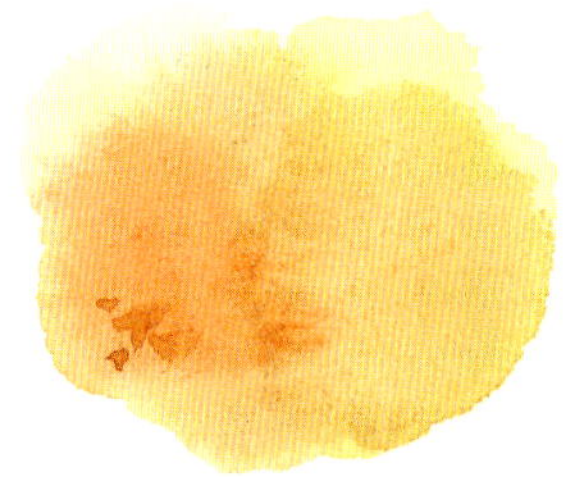

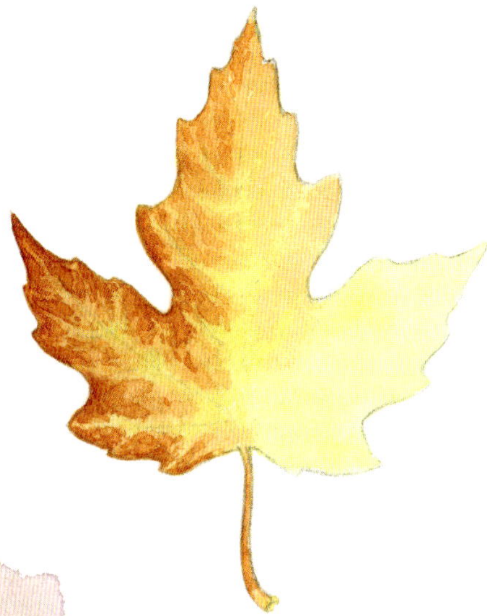

Wet-on-Dry

This technique consists of waiting until one color is dry before painting another over it. This will create clean lines and contours. Here, I applied an initial wash of Mauve and Burnt Umber. Once the color was dry, I applied a second wash in spots to make the shaded areas darker. After drying, I added the details with a fine brush.

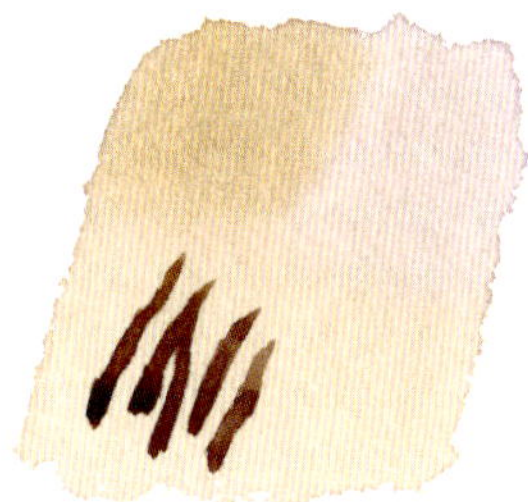

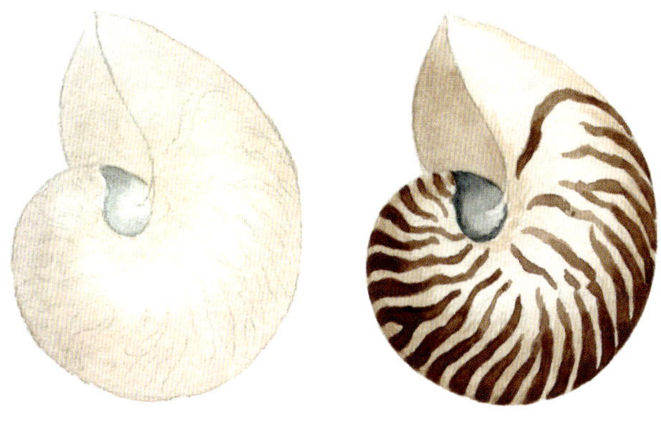

BASIC EXERCISES

Layering Colors

Colors:

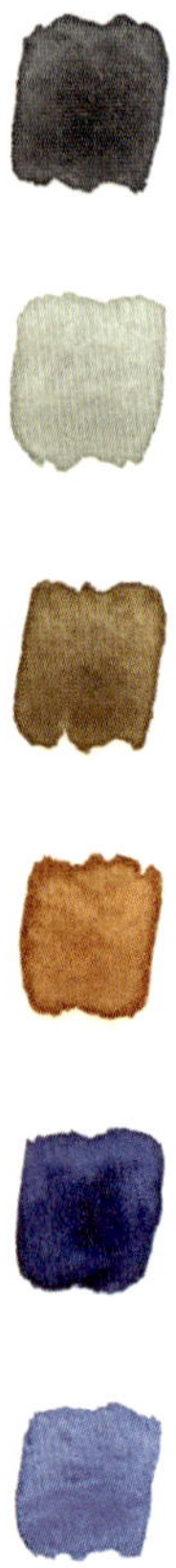

- Payne's Gray
- Davy's Gray
- Burnt Umber
- Burnt Sienna
- Prussian Blue
- Cerulean Blue

1. Generously moisten the surface of each feather, then add the first wash before the paper dries.

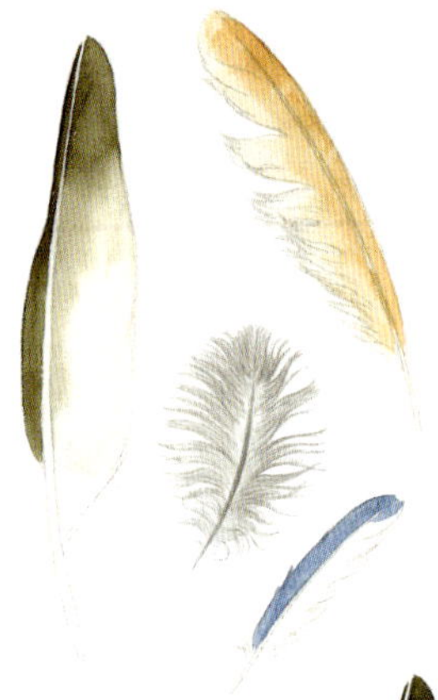

2. Moisten the two upper feathers again and add new touches of color. The hues will darken. Work the two smaller feathers in wet-on-dry.

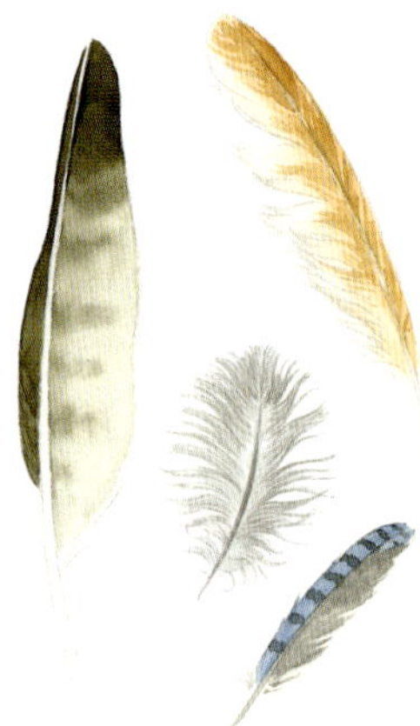

3. Increase the density of the hues with successive washes in wet-on-wet. Create the details using a fine brush and less diluted colors.

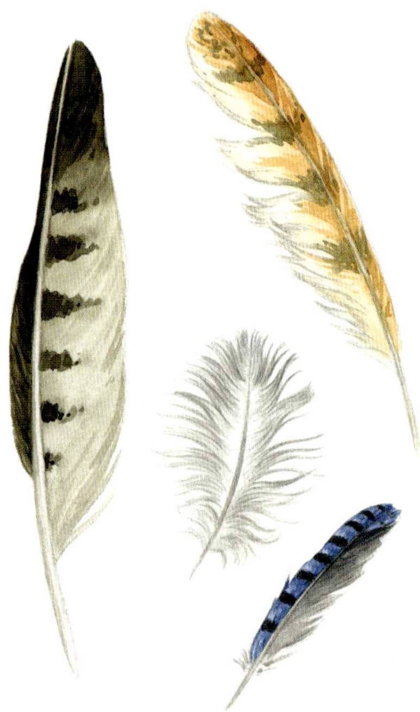

Reserving the White of the Paper

Colors:

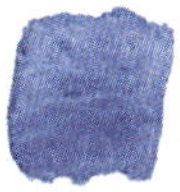

Cerulean Blue

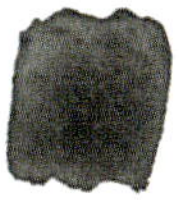

Payne's Gray

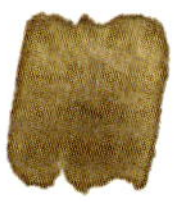

Burnt Umber

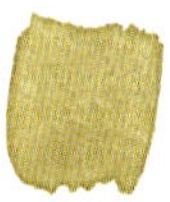

Raw Umber

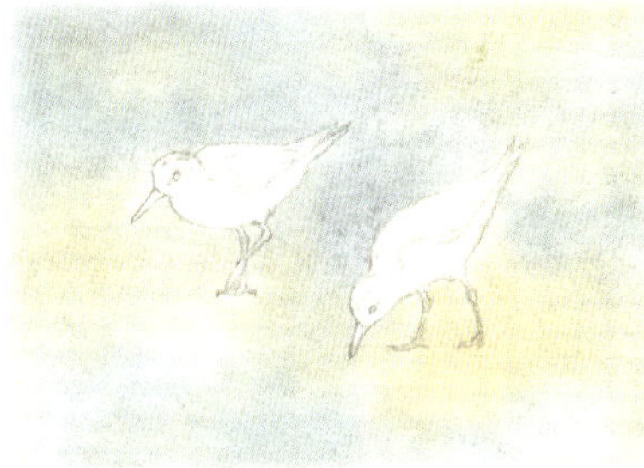

1. Generously moisten the background, carefully going around the contours of the birds. This will allow you to reserve the white of the paper for the birds. Then, alternately apply a mix of transparent Cerulean Blue and Payne's Gray, and diluted Raw Umber.

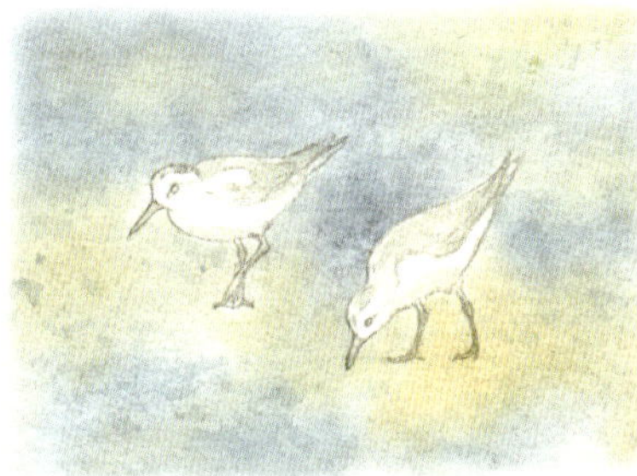

2. Partially moisten the birds, taking care to leave parts of them dry as shown, then apply a wash of Burnt Umber and Raw Umber on the wet parts. Let it dry.

3. Deepen the tones progressively, working in wet-on-dry.

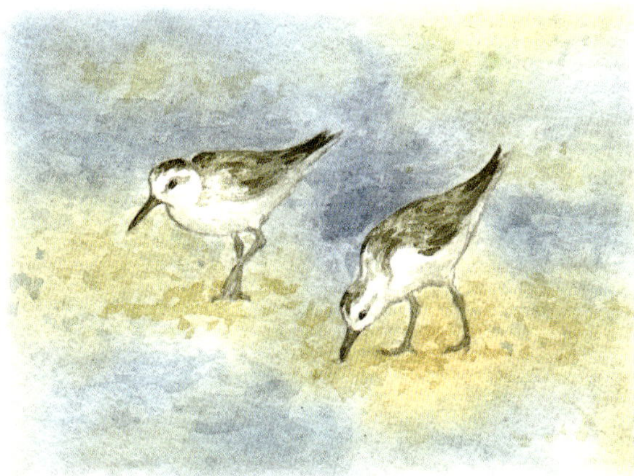

PLEIN AIR PAINTING

For both beginners and seasoned watercolorists, nothing compares to painting outdoors. When painting outside, bring minimal supplies. You can buy an empty watercolor box for carrying the colors you choose (in pans). These boxes come with a double cover, which serves as a palette. For simple sketches, a sketchbook will suffice. Back at home, work on watercolor paper, relying on your preparatory studies.

Many watercolorists don't bother with a box for working outdoors. Painting in the open air relies on grasping images quickly, without complicated techniques or effects. The fleeting nature of the subject (changing light, a bird in movement) requires you to convey the essentials in a few brushstrokes. It is up to you to determine what you want to capture: the fragility of a translucent petal, the abundance of colors in a bird's plumage, and so on. By focusing on the essentials, you will prioritize the very things that make watercolor so attractive: spontaneity and freshness.

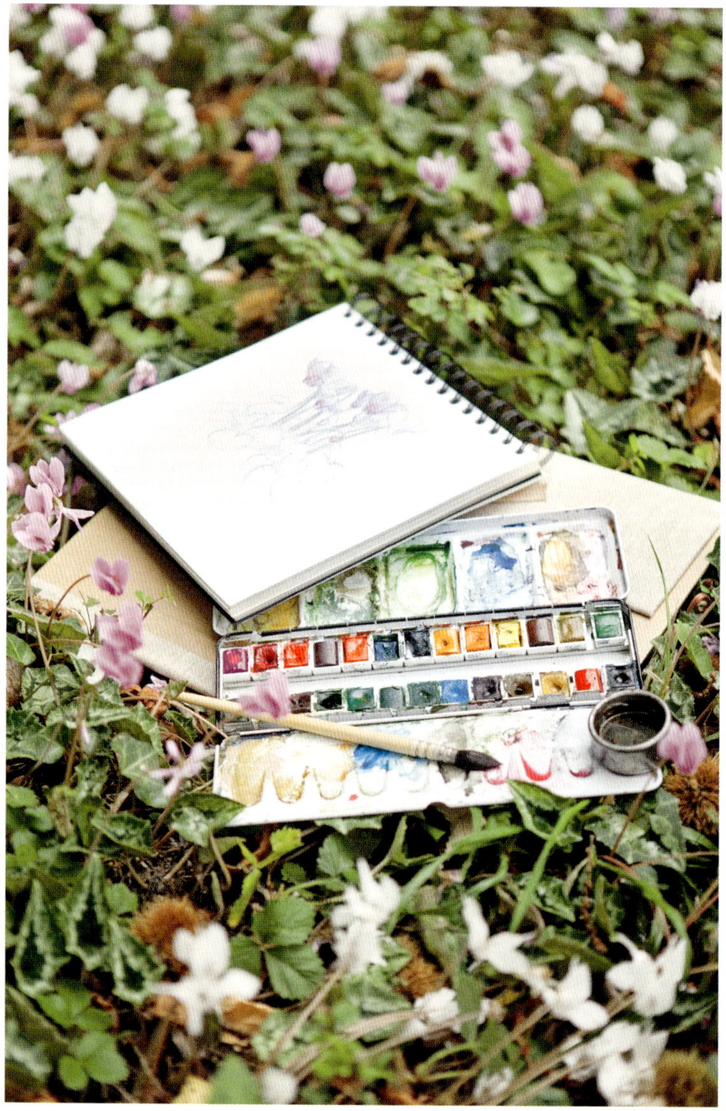

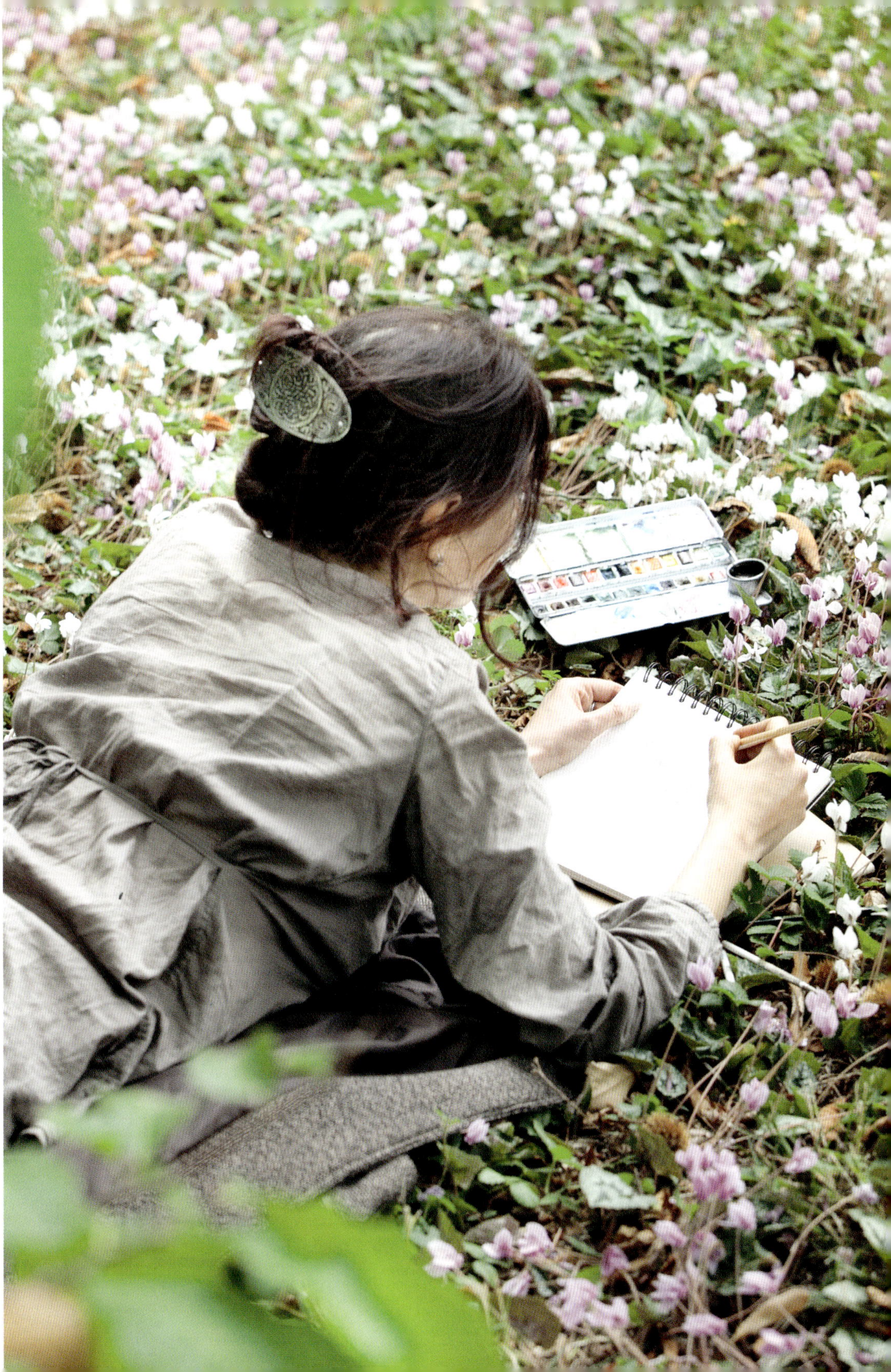

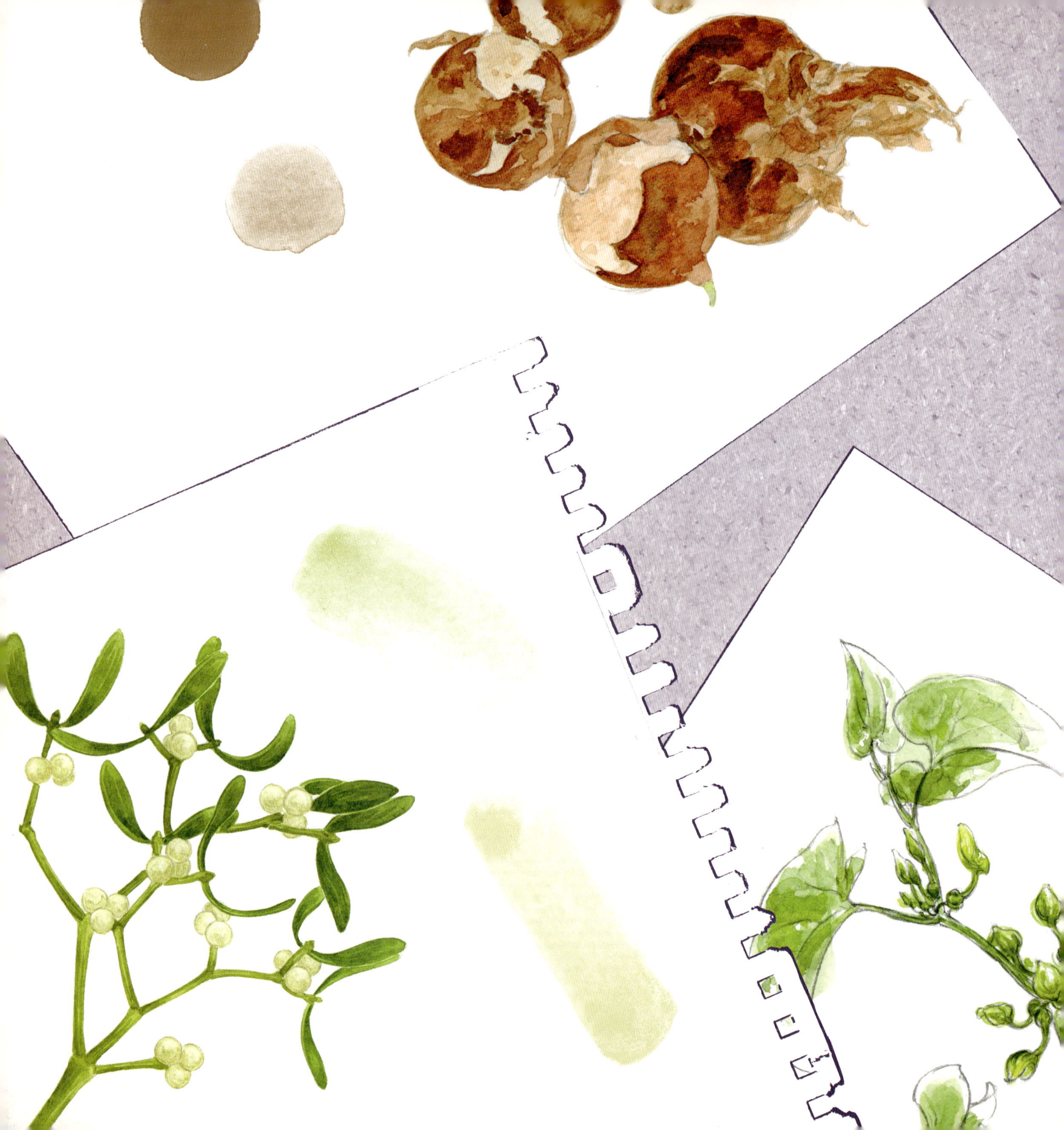

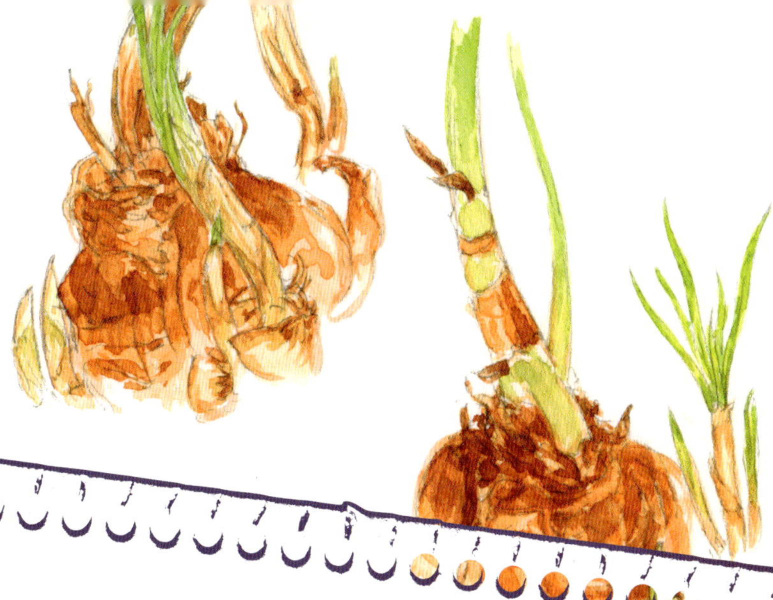

In Fields and Woods

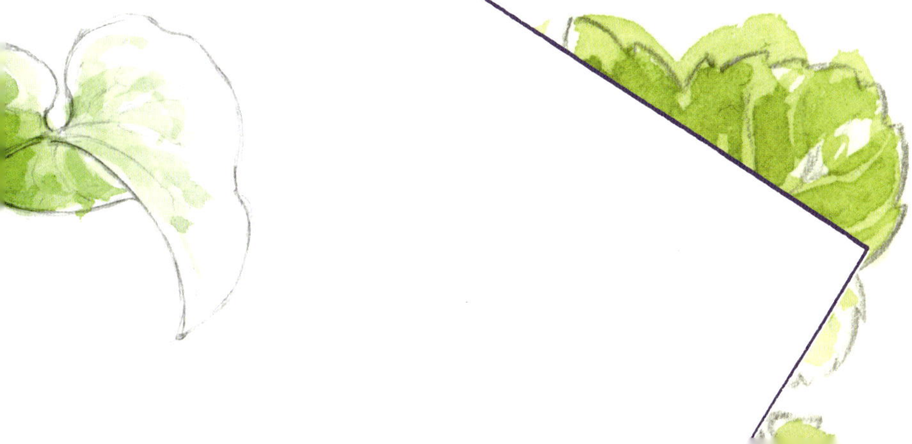

CROCUS

The delicate hues of these spring flowers are perfectly rendered with several layers of transparent washes.

Colors:

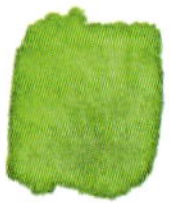
Sap Green

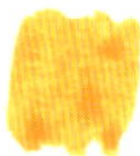
Indian Yellow

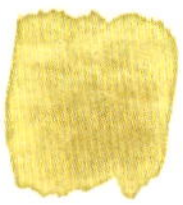
Yellow Ochre

Cadmium Yellow Light

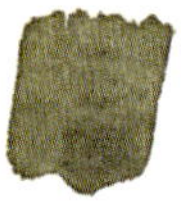
Sepia

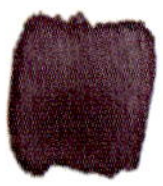
Permanent Mauve

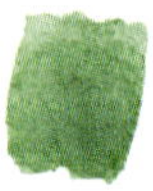
Emerald Green

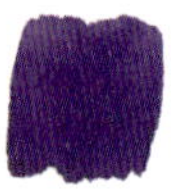
Dioxazine Purple

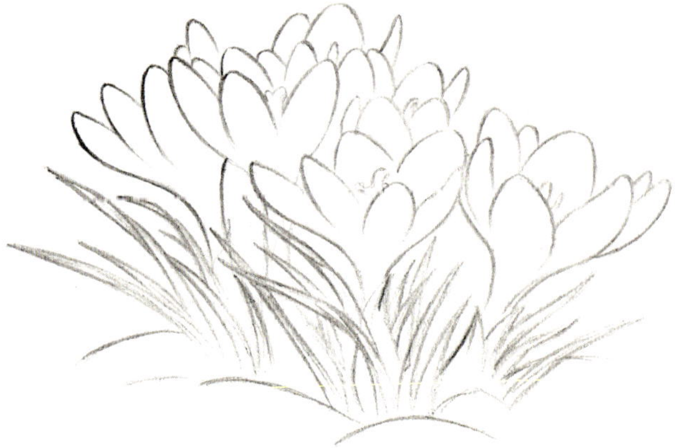

1. Draw the contours of the flowers, leaves, and surface of the soil. Feel free to make the leaves a bit disorderly, counterbalancing the smooth regularity of the crocus.

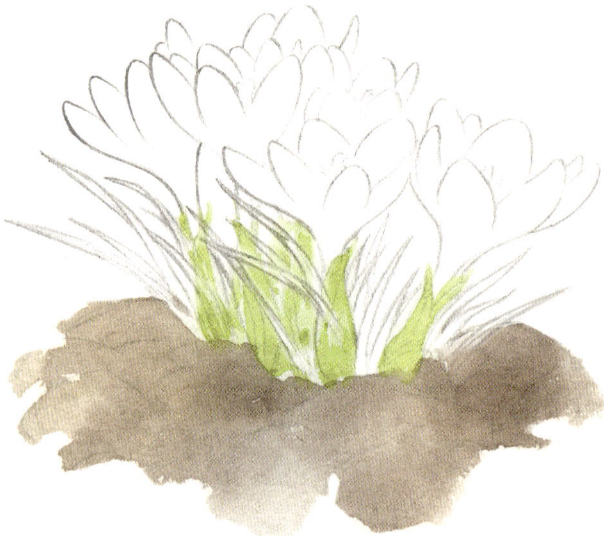

2. On the visible parts of the bulbs, apply a light mixture of Sap Green and Yellow Ochre. Then paint the soil using a mix of Sepia and Mauve

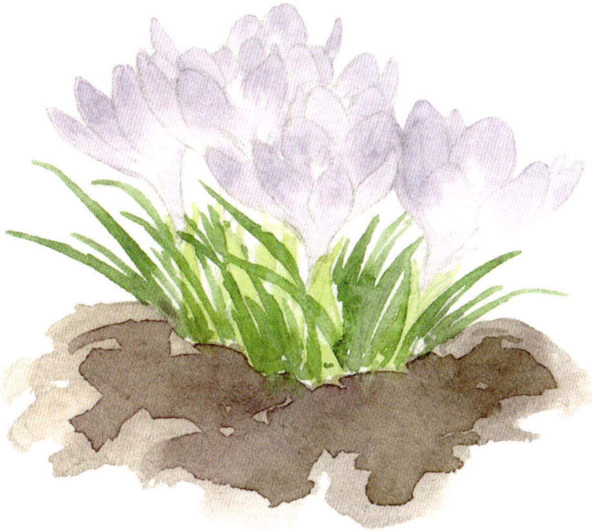

3. Next, paint the leaves smoothly with a mix of Sap Green, Emerald Green, and Sepia. Then moisten the petals and apply a very diluted mix of Dioxazine Purple and Sepia. Do not try to achieve a perfect hue with this first layer; the accumulation of washes will gradually produce the desired tone.

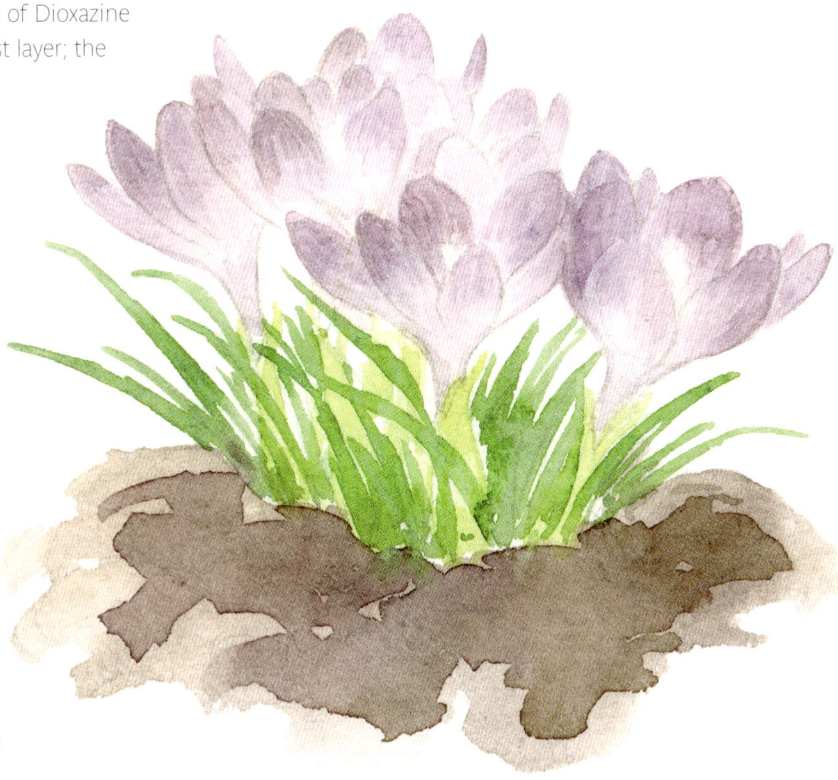

4. The earth becomes denser with a second, deeper-hued wash of Sepia and Mauve. Do not cover it entirely. Next, apply a second wash on the petals, using a very fine brush; leave long thin areas unpainted to indicate veins and ribs.

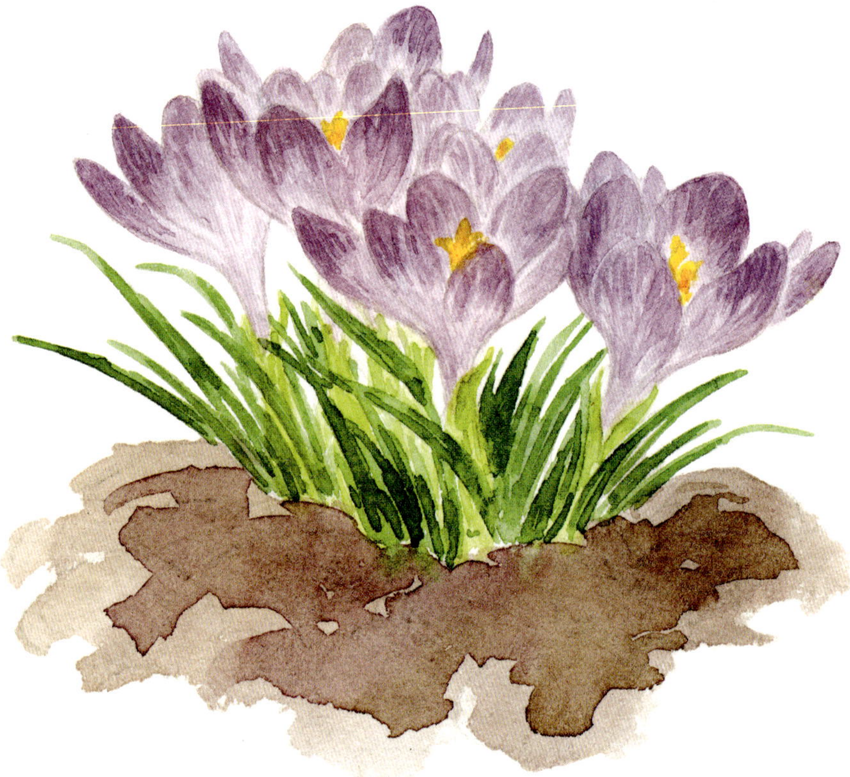

5. Finish the corolla of petals with a final, deeper-hued wash over the lighter washes. Make sure never to completely cover the preceding coat. Accent the shading of the leaves with the help of a mixture of Sap Green, Emerald Green, and Sepia. Add a touch of Indian Yellow and Cadmium Yellow Light on the pistils.

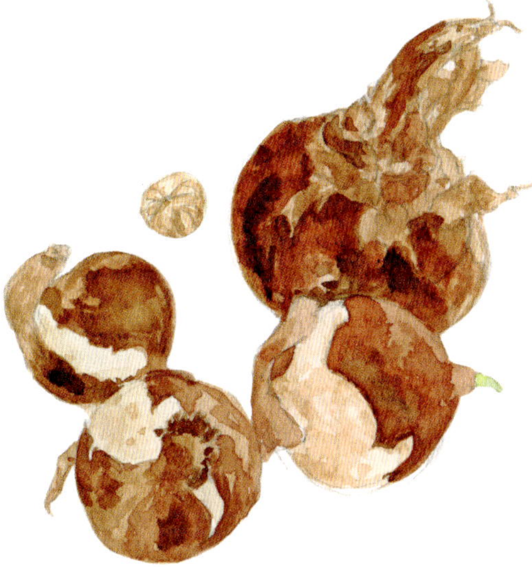

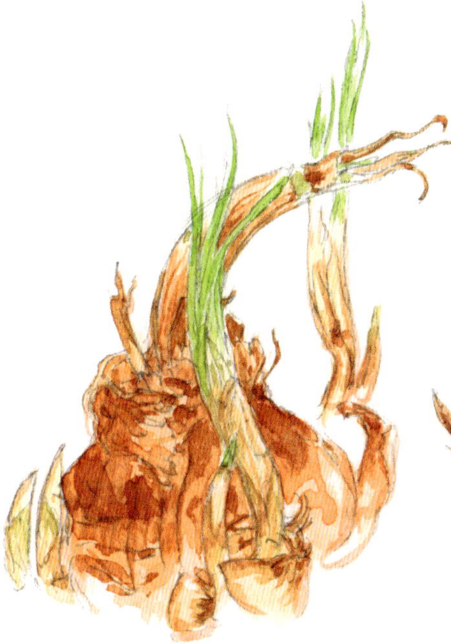

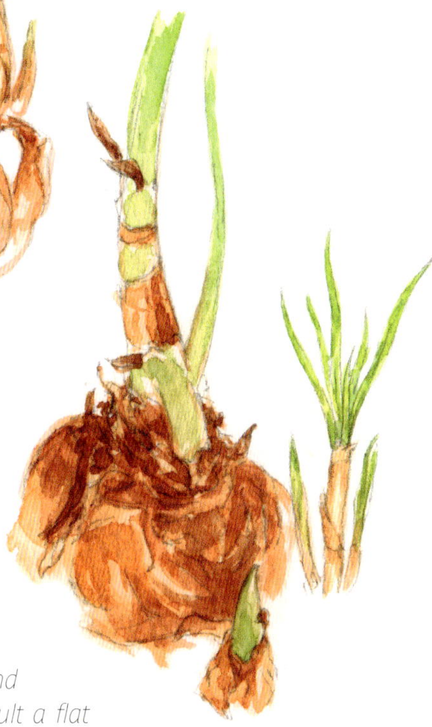

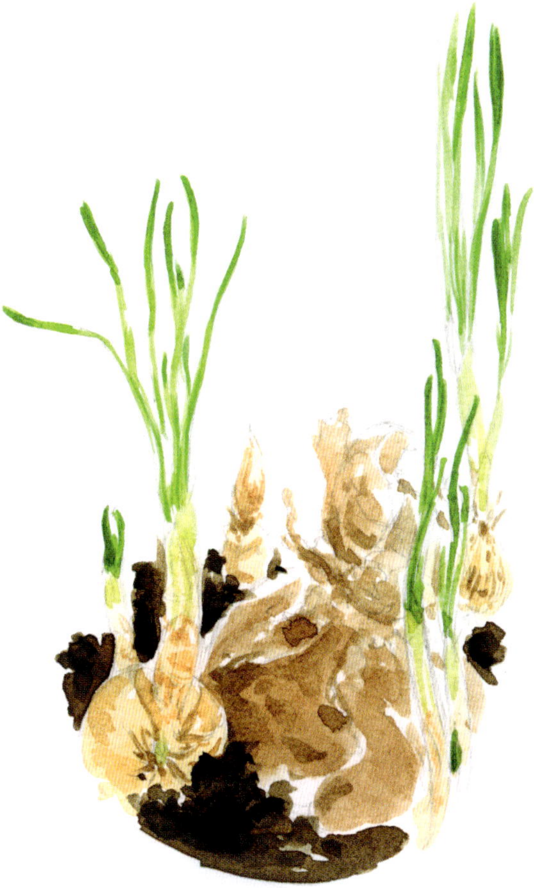

Bulbs

The underground part of bulbs is an excellent subject for study. Layer washes of color with swift touches, as you would for the bark of a tree.

Avoid making the contours too clean and precise so that you don't give the result a flat quality.

You can make certain colors (to the left, the earth) denser in order to achieve powerful contrasts, but be careful to reserve the white of the paper in various spots. The contrasts will be stronger for it and the watercolor more luminous.

BRAMBLE FLOWERS

This stalk of brambles allows you to render both the velvety appearance of the forming buds and the fragility of the pale pink flowers, similar to wild roses. You can complete this study in three stages, freely painting beyond the lines of your pencil sketch.

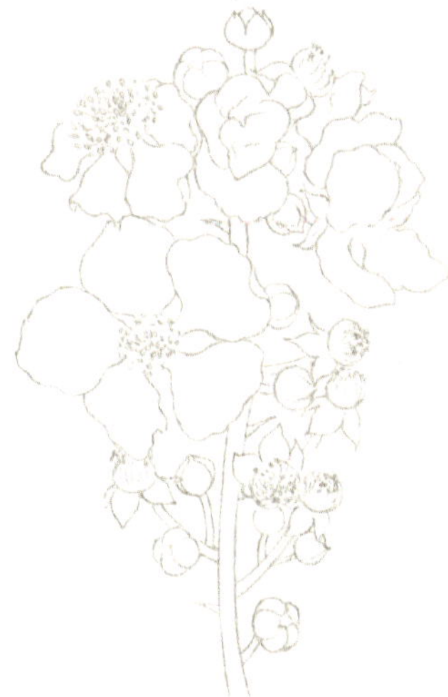

1. Rapidly draw the stalk with flowers and buds. Don't simplify the petals too much. Their crumpled look will give them more subtle delicacy.

Colors:

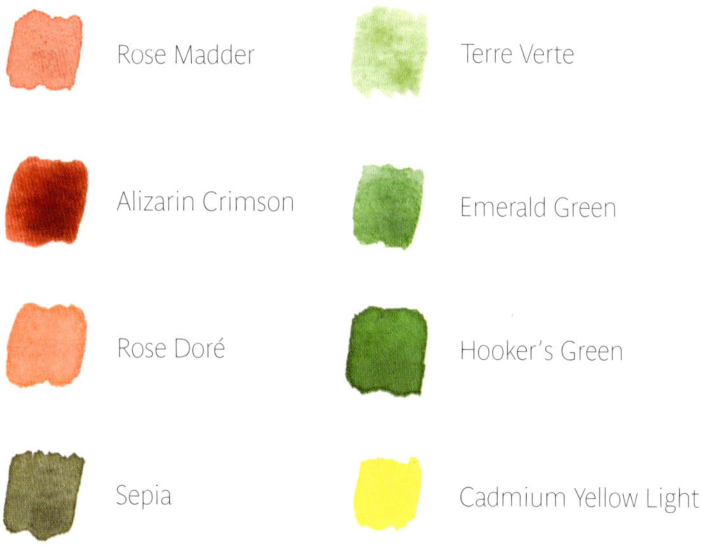

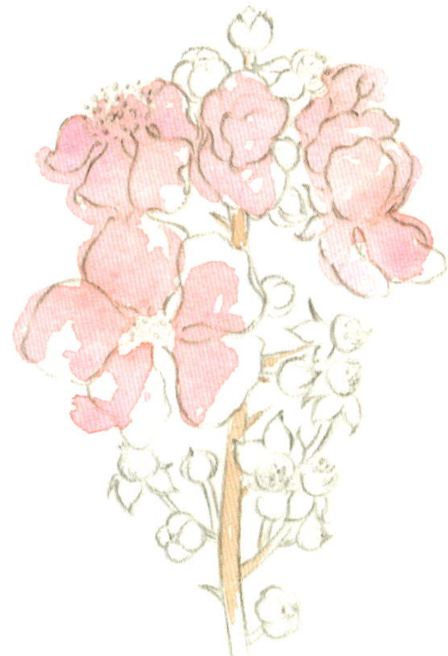

2. Prepare a diluted mixture of Rose Madder, Alizarin Crimson, and Rose Doré, and apply it smoothly to the petals. Go over the stalk with a wash of Sepia and Rose Madder. Don't try to "color" each petal, but rather to convey the lightness of the flowers, reserving the white of the paper in places.

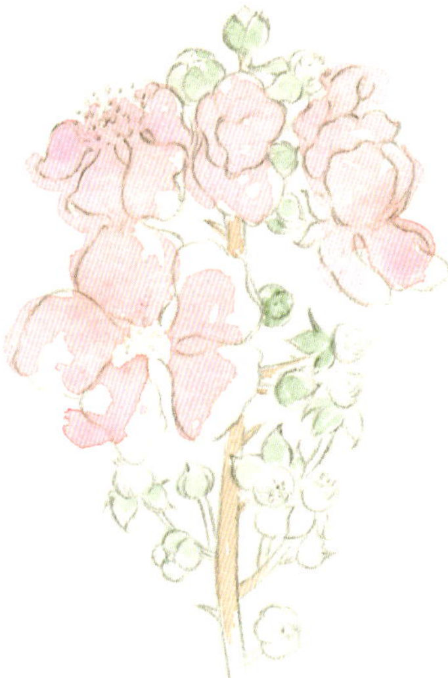

3. Apply a mixture of Terre Verte, Emerald Green, and Hooker's Green to the buds and calyxes.

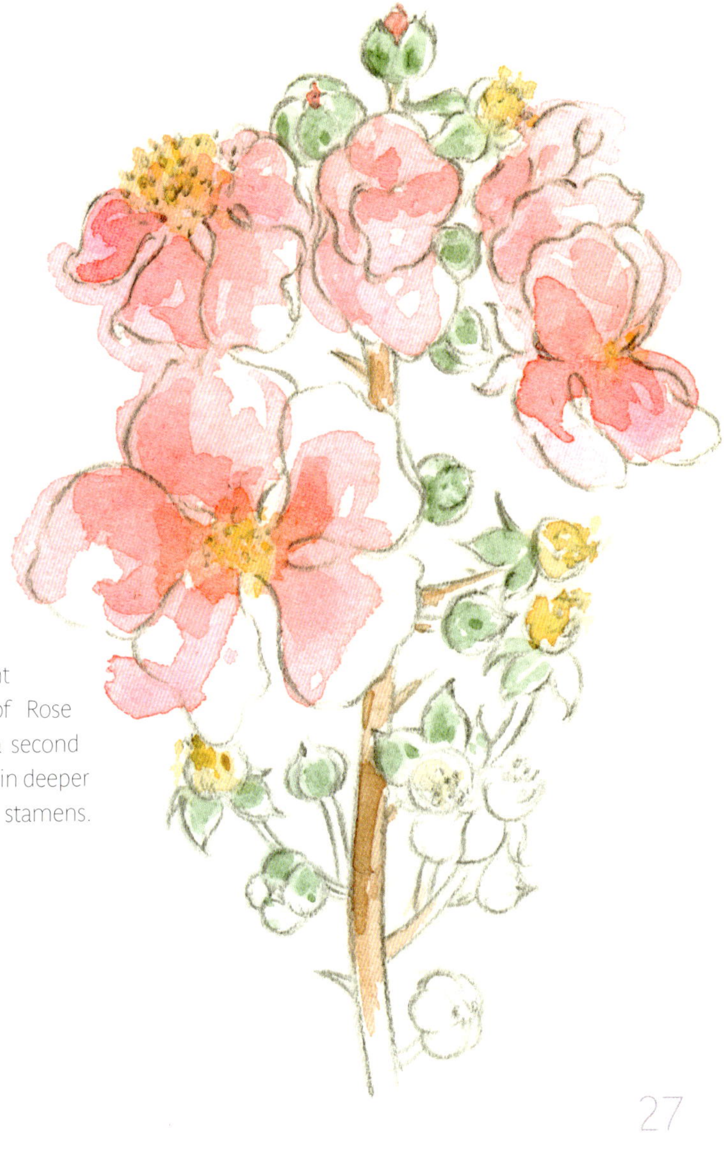

4. Moisten the stamens and apply a mixture of Cadmium Yellow Light and Rose Doré to them. Immediately apply a second wash of Rose Madder, Alizarin Crimson, and Rose Doré to the petals. Then add a second wash on the stem and the buds, using the same mixtures as before but in deeper hues. Add tiny touches of Cadmium Yellow Light and Rose Doré to the stamens.

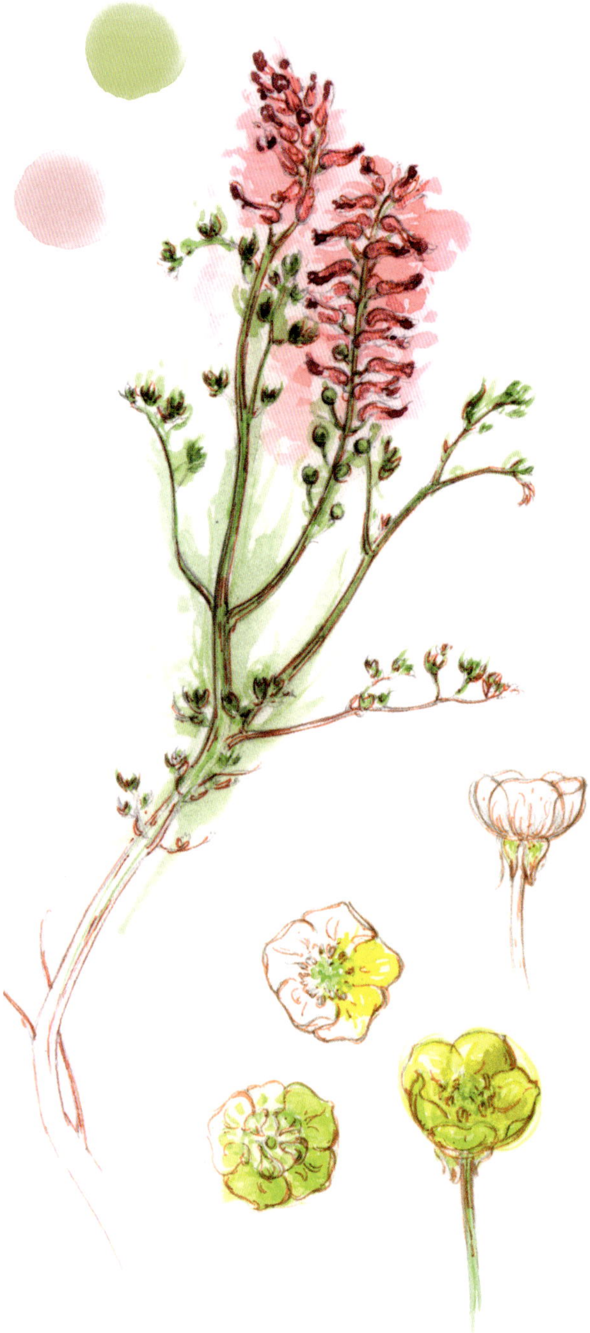

Wildflowers

By painting freely and liberally beyond the confines of the flowers' contours, you will give the colors more impact. This technique is especially suited to minuscule subjects (here, on the left, a sprig of fumitory flowers). In observing these small bell flowers, I was struck by the intensity of their colors, which is why I let the watercolor washes burst beyond the contours. One must dare to transcend reality in order to reproduce the force of an impression.

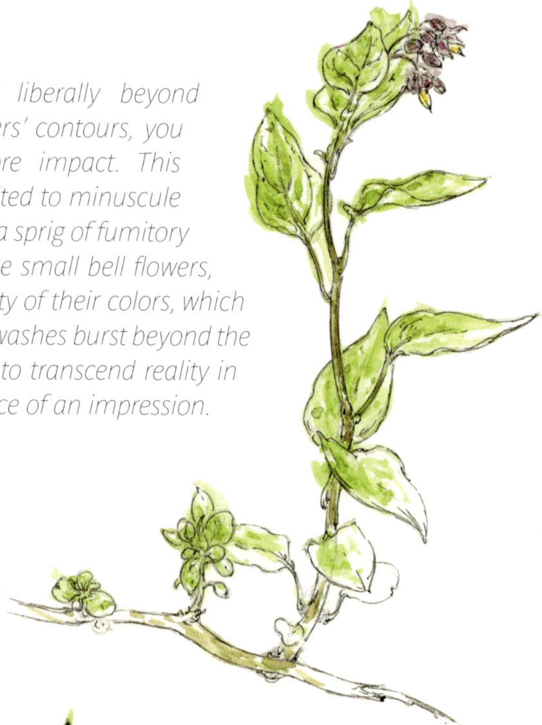

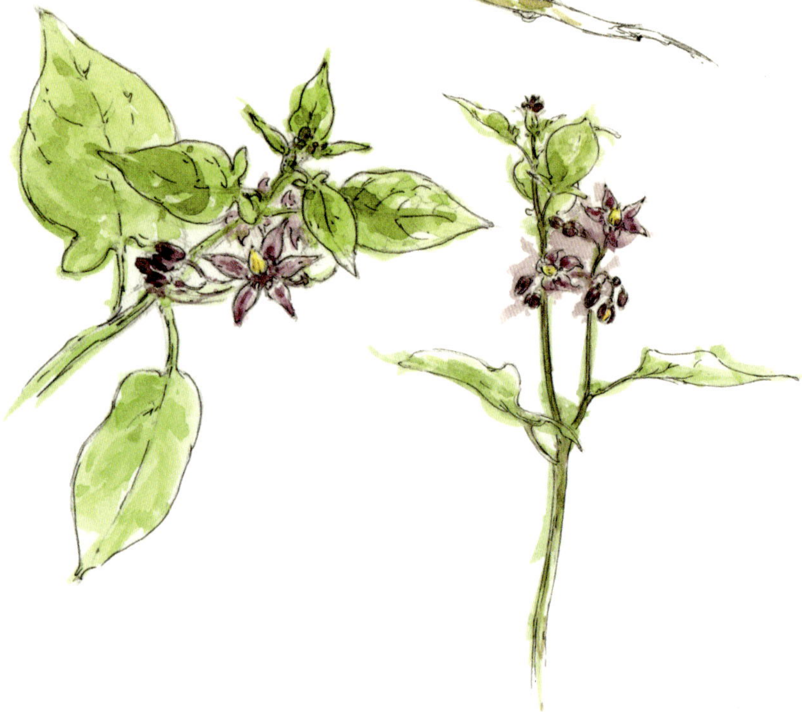

MISTLETOE

Even in the heart of winter, nature offers the watercolorist magnificent subjects, as long as one knows how to observe…

You will find mistletoe in wooded areas and can easily cut off a few branches to paint them indoors.

Colors:

Yellow Ochre

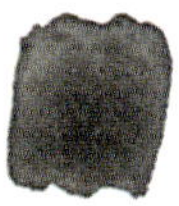

Davy's Gray

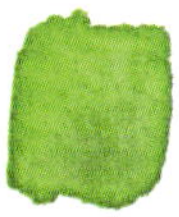

Sap Green

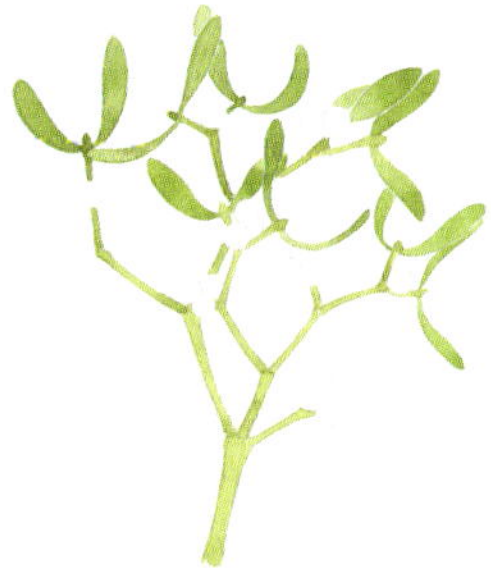

1. Moisten the leaves, then apply a dilute mixture of Sap Green, Yellow Ochre, and Davy's Gray to them. Paint the stems a similar color but with more Yellow Ochre in it.

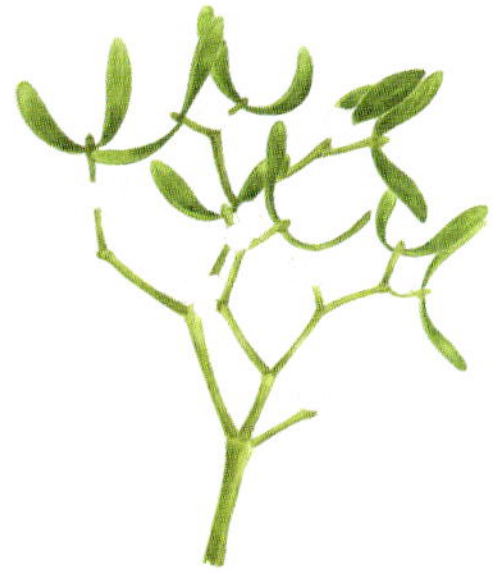

2. Mark the shadows and ribs of the leaves and stems using the same mixtures as before but in deeper shades.

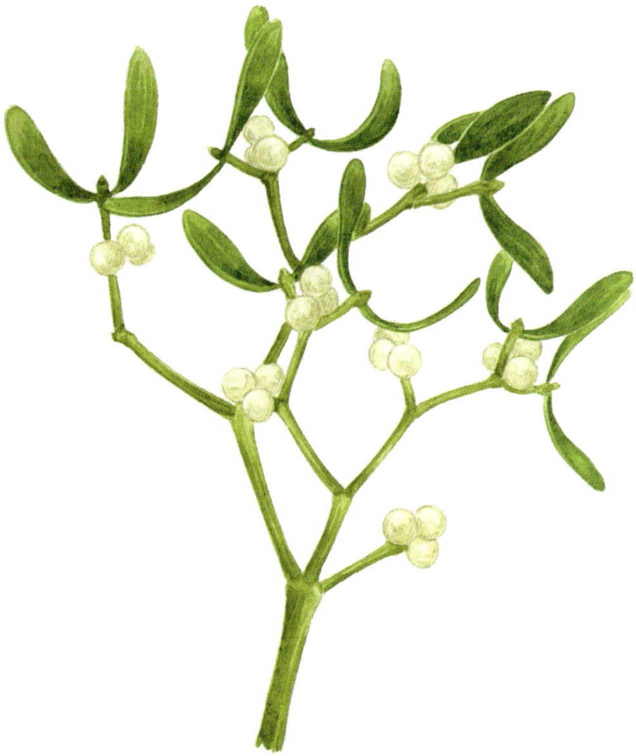

3. The berries are not really white, but rather a subtle light hue that you can create using a mixture of Yellow Ochre and Davy's Gray. Moisten the berries, then apply this mixture to them in a very diluted form, using small irregular touches. Once this has dried thoroughly, apply a second wash in the same manner.

SWEET PEA

Sweet pea grows along embankments as well as in the garden. A bright pink or pastel pink, its fine petals allow light to show through, an effect that watercolor can render beautifully.

Colors:

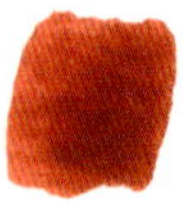
Alizarin Crimson

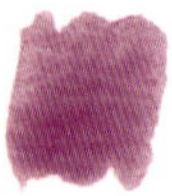
Cobalt Violet

Permanent Mauve

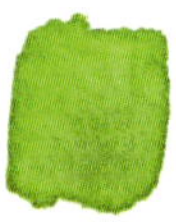
Sap Green

Emerald Green

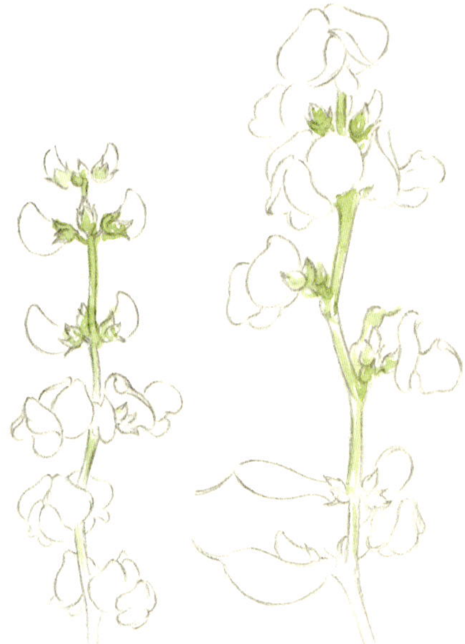

1. Prepare a light wash of Sap Green mixed with Emerald Green and apply it lightly on the stems.

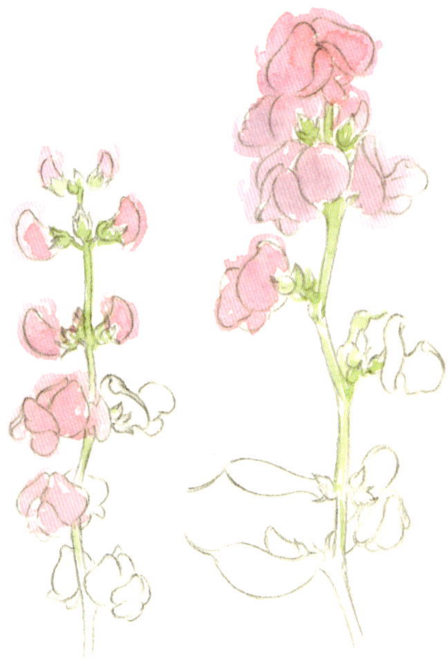

2. Apply a wash of Alizarin Crimson and Cobalt Violet to some of the flowers, adding a dash of Mauve to a few of them; not all the flowers are the same color. Don't worry about going past the contours of your drawing.

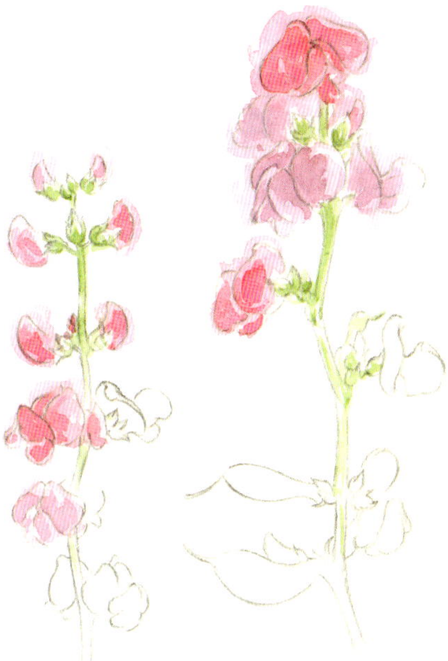

3. Accentuate these colors with a second wash, denser in color but of the same mix, being careful this time to stay within the borders of your drawing. Mark the edge of the stem with a brushstroke of Emerald Green mixed with Sap Green.

4. Emphasize the shaded areas of the flowers on top with a final wash, only slightly diluted, using the original mix of colors.

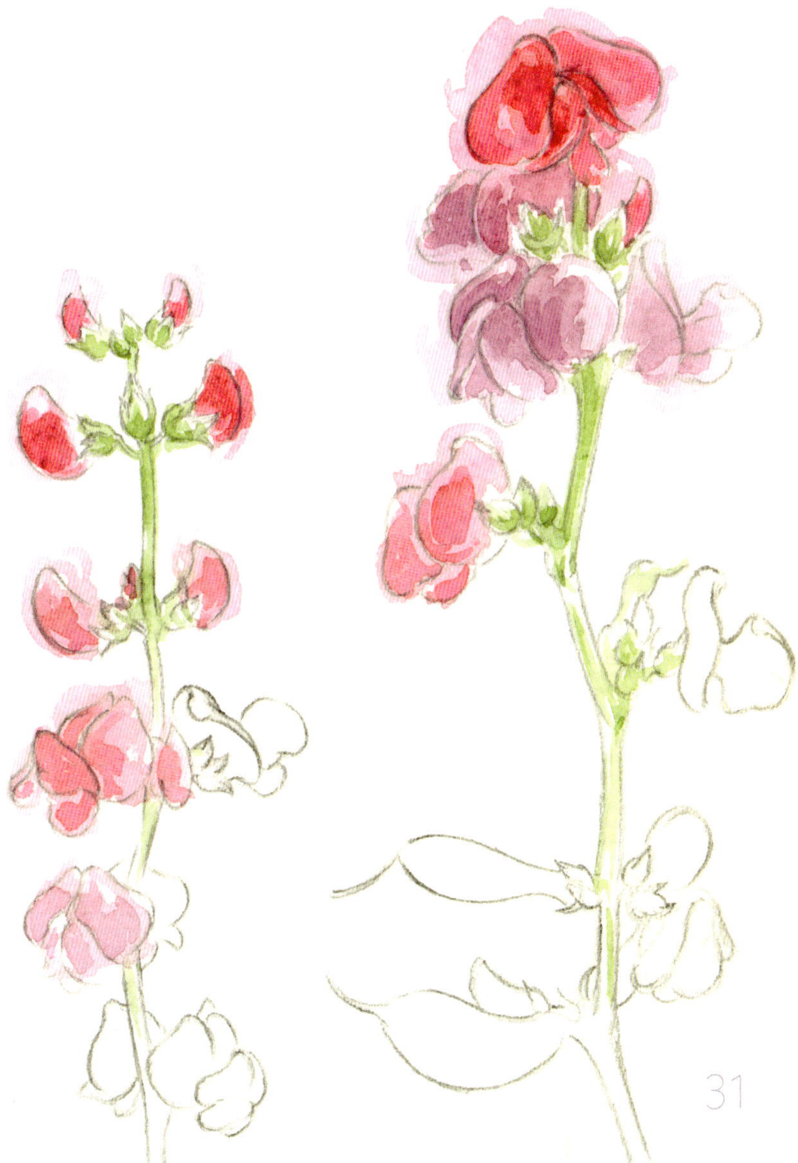

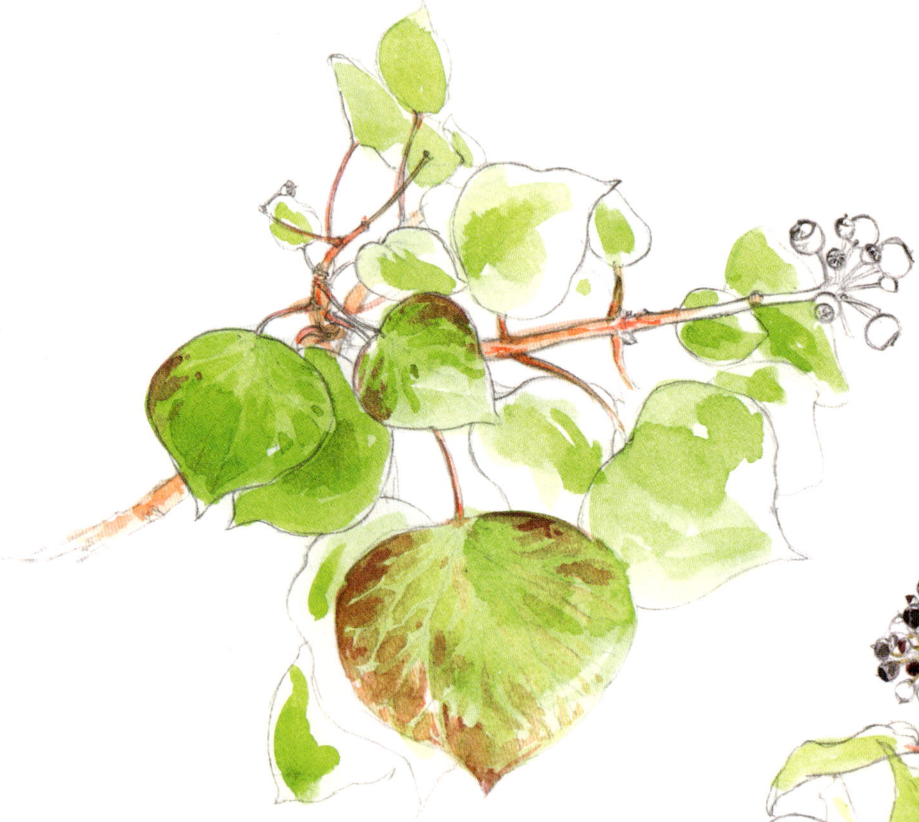

Leaves and Berries

To draw attention to one component, you may wish to de-emphasize another. Here, I have emphasized the berries in one painting, and the leaves in the other. On the right, the berries are a darker color. Above, the study emphasizes the leaves, whose nuances would have been weakened if the berries were too prominent.

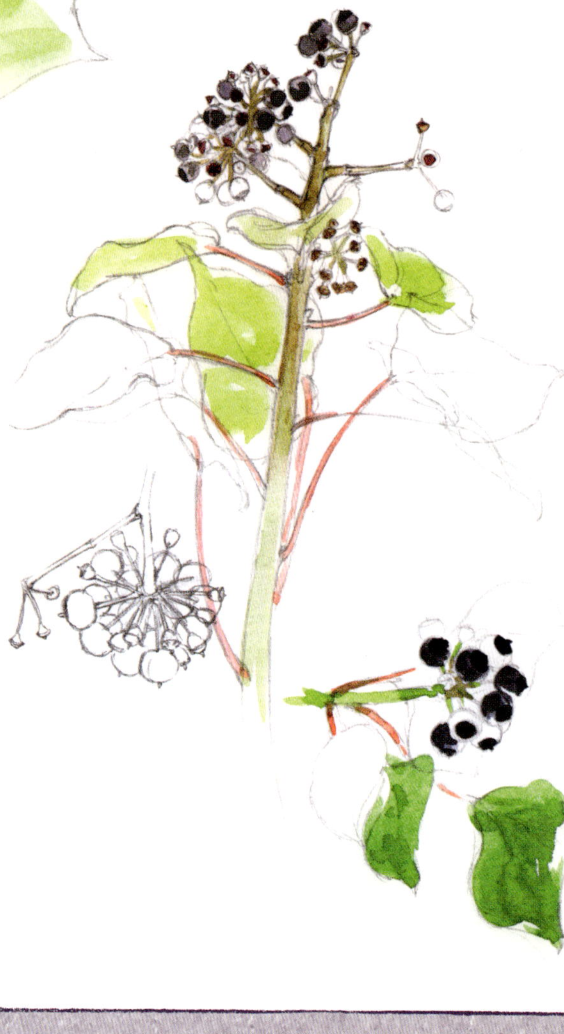

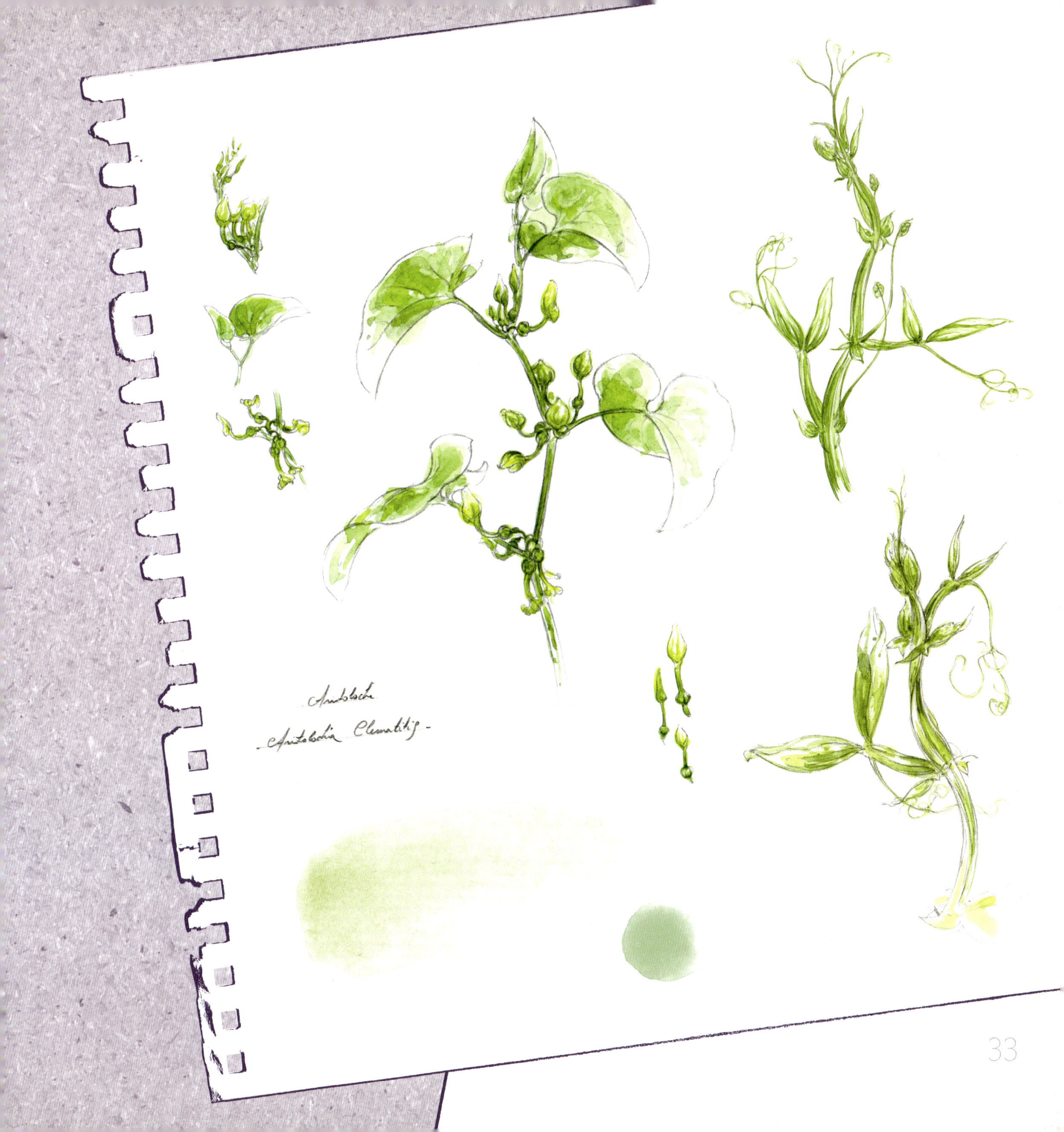
Aristoloche
- Aristolochia Clematitis -

REDCURRANT

Wild berries are little gems for the contemplation of the artist. The dazzling colors and shine of redcurrants are highly suited to watercolor.

Colors:

 Cadmium Yellow Light

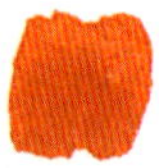 Cadmium Red Deep

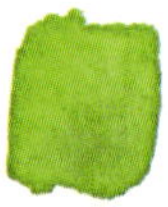 Sap Green

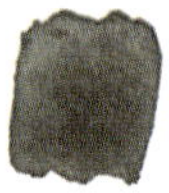 Payne's Gray

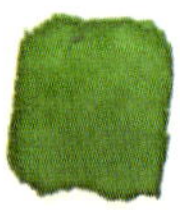 Hooker's Green

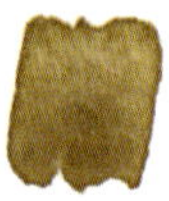 Burnt Umber

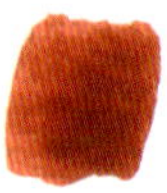 Alizarin Crimson

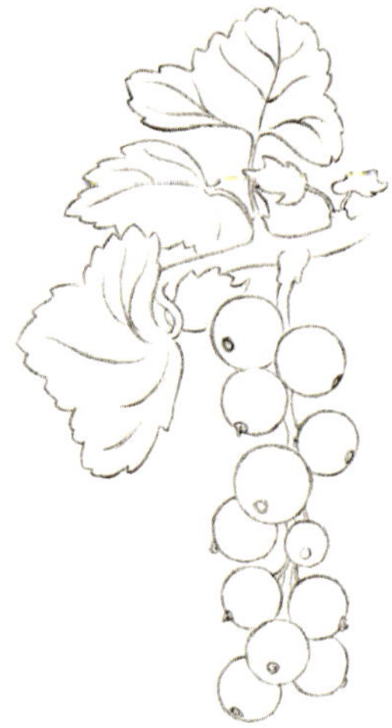

1. Quickly sketch the branch and cluster of redcurrants. The fruits should be perfectly round, while the branch or the leaves can show some irregularities.

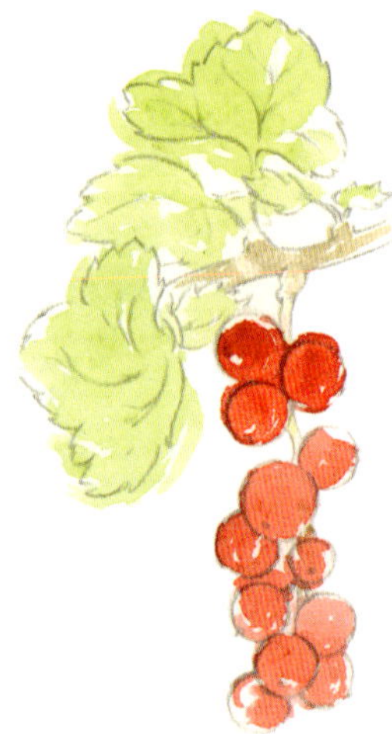

2. Apply a mixture of Cadmium Yellow Light, Sap Green, and Hooker's Green on the leaves, using brushstrokes that follow the shape of the leaves. On the stem, apply a wash of Burnt Umber with a dash of Alizarin Crimson, then give the berries a few touches of a diluted mixture of Alizarin Crimson and Cadmium Red Deep. Reserve some areas of white.

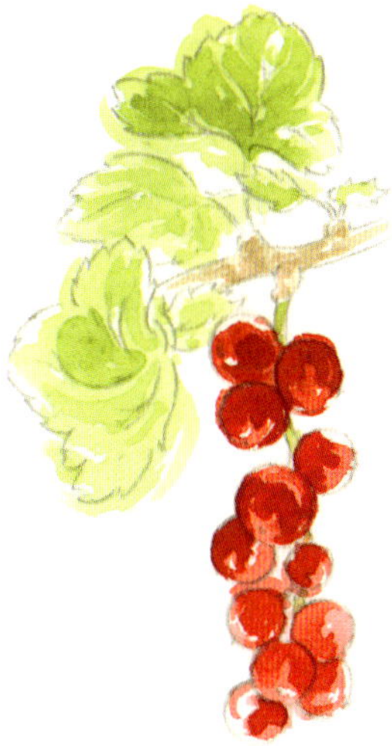

3. Give the berries dimension with a second wash of the same mixture but more intense, using small circular strokes. Also apply a denser wash of Sap Green and Cadmium Yellow Light on the stem and the leaves farthest away, leaving spaces clear for the veins. Give the branch a bit more presence by again applying a few slashes of Burnt Umber and Alizarin Crimson.

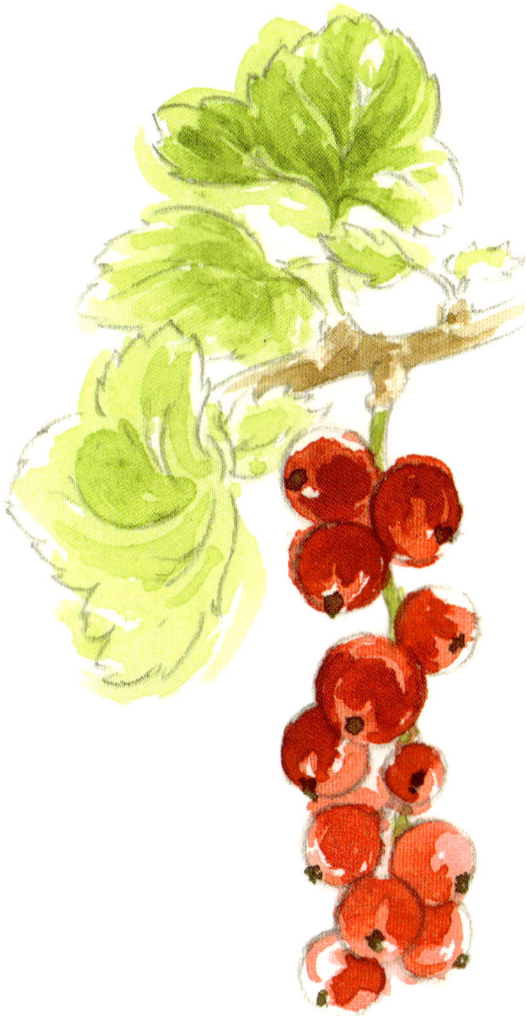

4. With a fine brush, add the little dark points of the redcurrants, using a mix of Payne's Gray and Burnt Umber—not too dense, so as to avoid "eclipsing" the other hues.

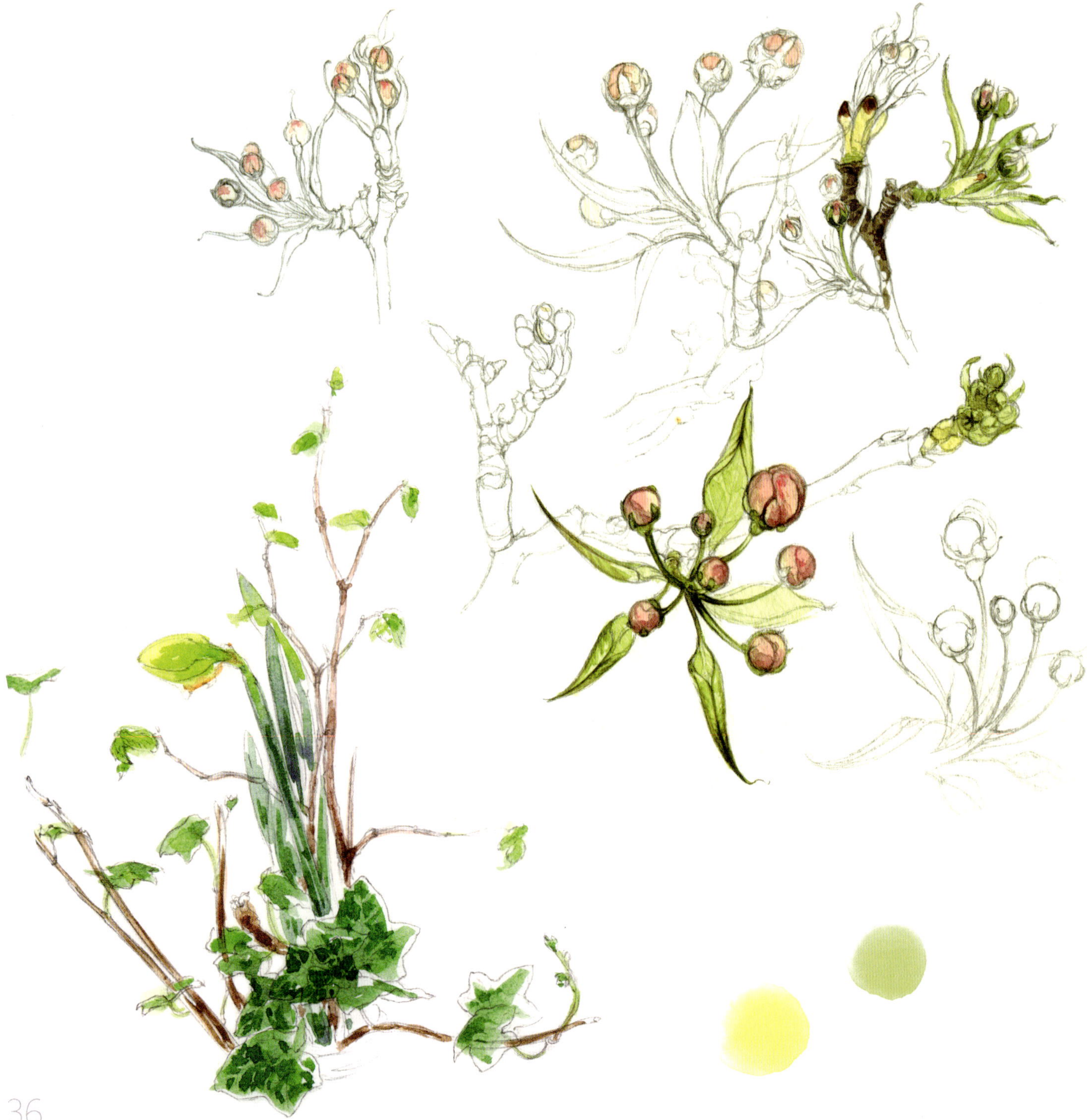

Buds and Flowers

In blooming season you can see flowers in every stage, from first buds to mature blossoms. By proceeding methodically from bud to flower in full bloom, you will be better able to understand the rustle of petals, how they are attached to the stem, and the way in which the green envelope of the bud opens up. Each step leads to another.

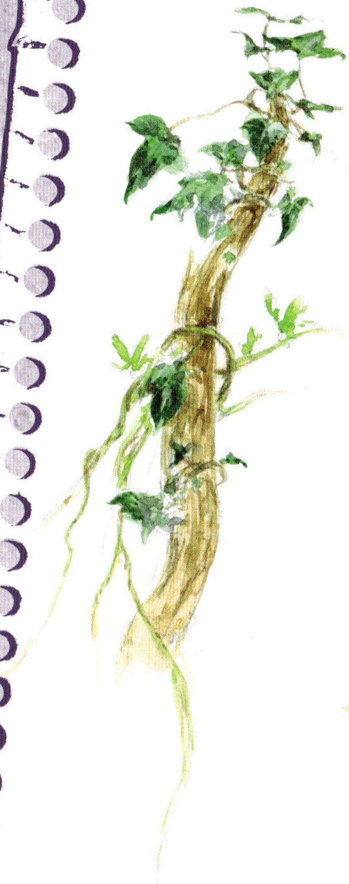

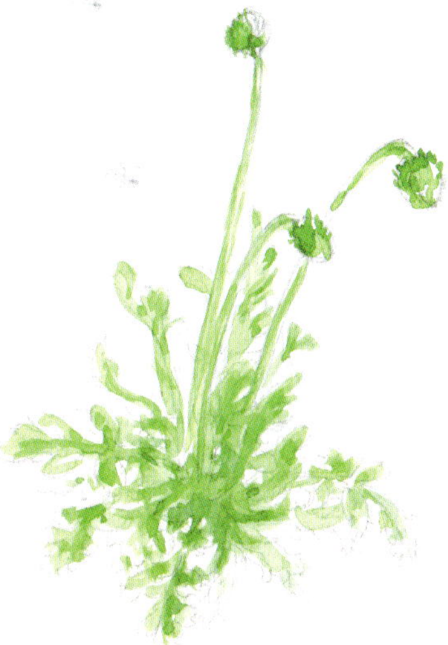

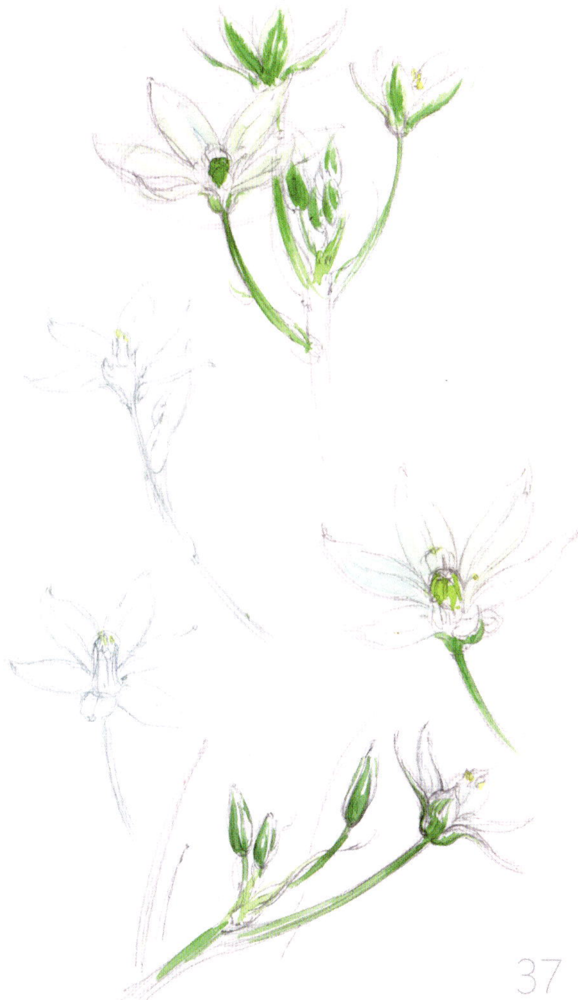

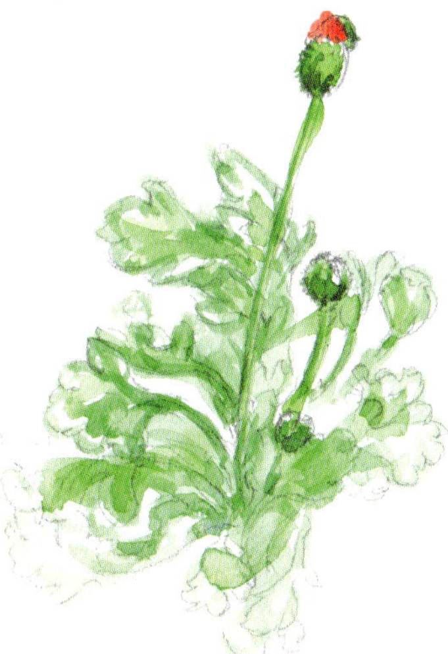

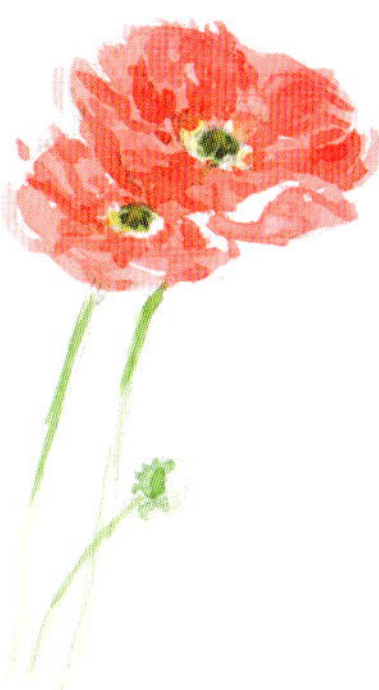

TREE AND MISTLETOE

This tree with intertwined branches owes its graceful allure to multiple bushes of mistletoe covering it. Their characteristically gentle shapes are best rendered with a wet-on-wet technique, while the stark appearance of the tree that supports them should be worked wet-on-dry.

Colors:

Ultramarine Blue

Raw Umber

Payne's Gray

Sepia

Sap Green

Yellow Ochre

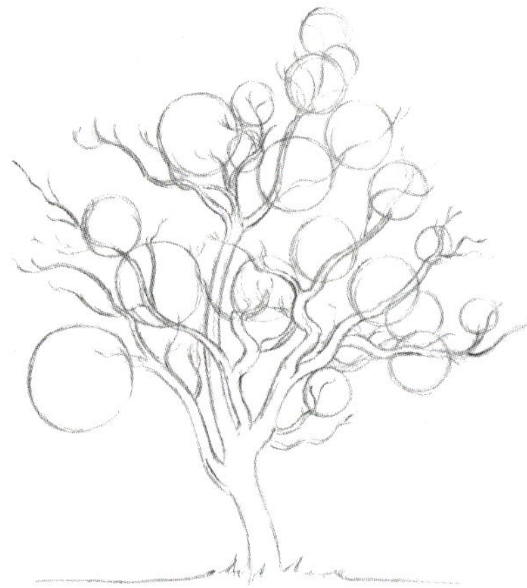

1. Rapidly sketch the silhouette of the tree, then place the masses of mistletoe bushes.

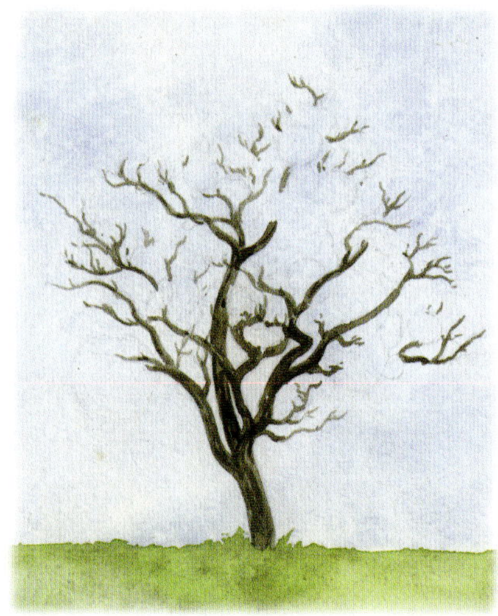

2. Moisten the sky area of the paper and apply a very diluted wash of Ultramarine Blue and Payne's Gray. When the wash has dried, do the same for the grass, using a very light mixture of Sap Green, Ultramarine Blue, and Raw Umber. Next, paint the trunk and branches with a mixture of Sepia and Payne's Gray. Then, mark the shadows with brushstrokes of the same mixture in a denser form. Leave the spaces for the mistletoe bushes blank.

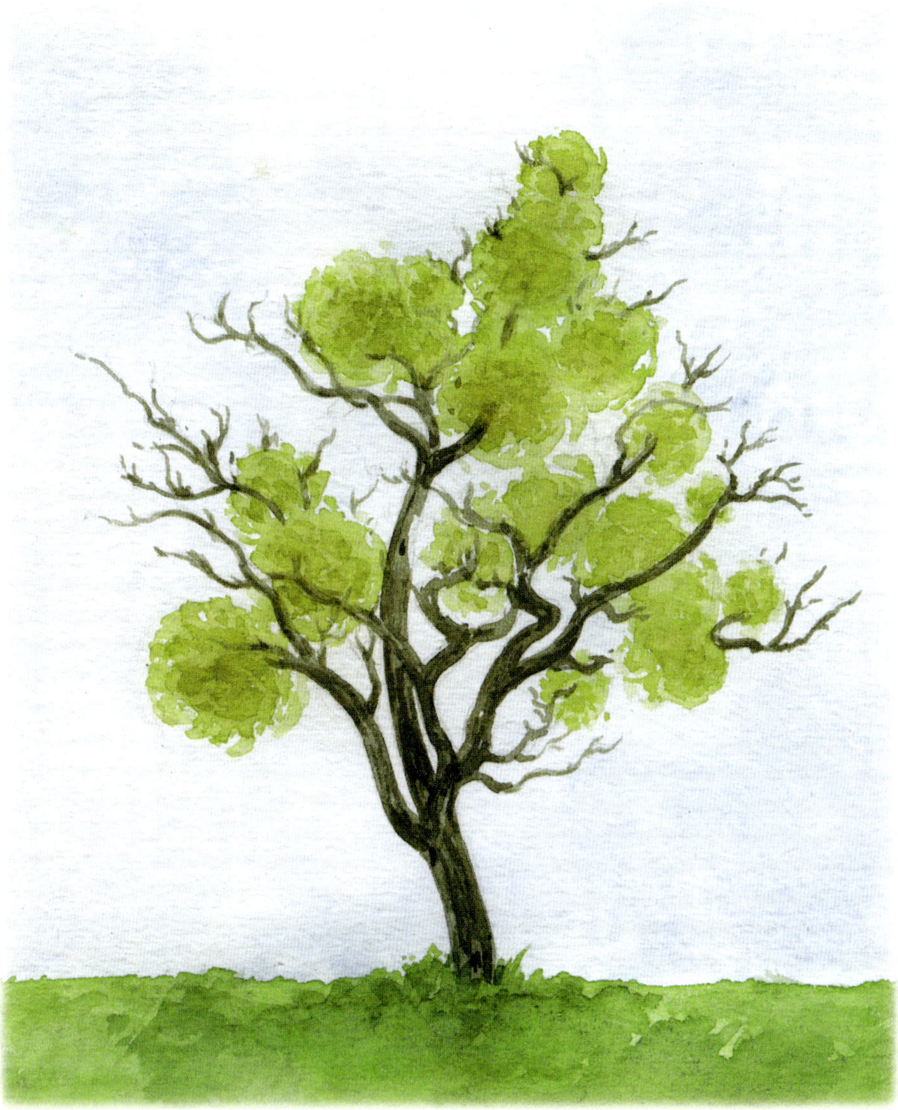

3. Moisten the areas where you will place the bushes, doing groups of four at a time so that the paper does not dry before you can apply the color. Do not moisten uniformly but rather in small touches; then in the same manner apply, in wet-on-wet, a mixture of Yellow Ochre, Sap Green, and Raw Umber. With small touches, apply a wash of Sap Green, Ultramarine Blue, and Raw Umber to the surrounding grass.

CHESTNUT LEAF

Autumn offers a variety of enchanting colors. Rusty gold, ochres, and reds compete with each other in the foliage. Here, a study of a fallen leaf presents spectacular chromatic effects.

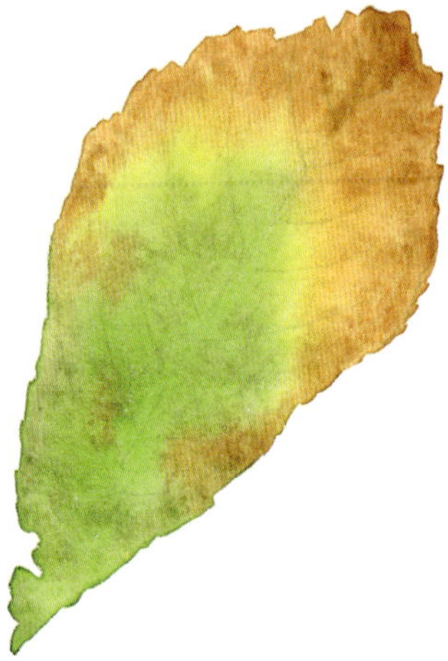

1. Moisten the paper liberally, then apply a wash of Sap Green and Burnt Umber on the lower part of the leaf. Place spots of Cadmium Yellow Light and Indian Yellow all around the green, and paint the contours of the upper section with a mixture of Burnt Sienna and Burnt Umber.

Colors:

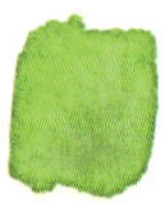
Sap Green

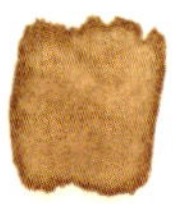
Burnt Sienna

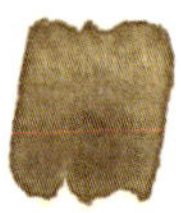
Burnt Umber

Cadmium Yellow Light

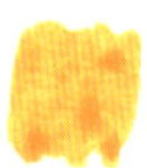
Indian Yellow

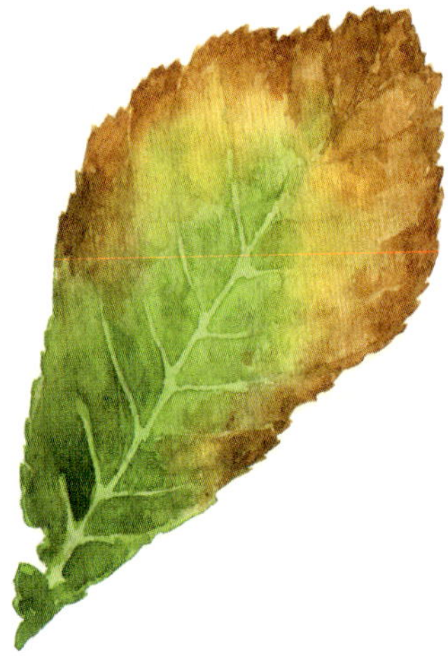

2. Apply a second wash using the same mixtures in denser form. Add the main veins of the leaf by leaving the lighter color of the previous washes where they are.

3. Darken the green by adding more Burnt Umber. Go over the veins with a light wash.

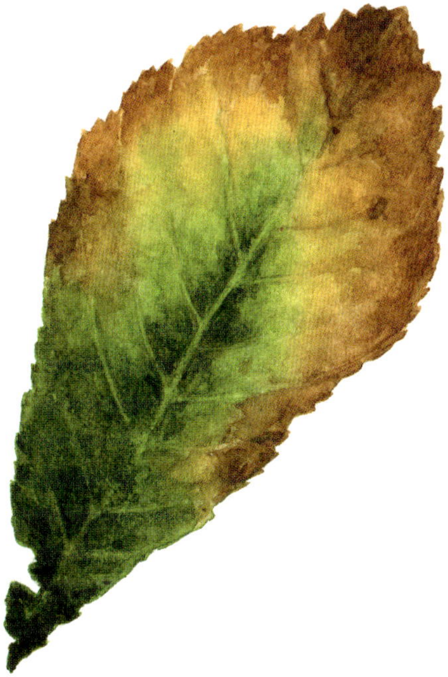

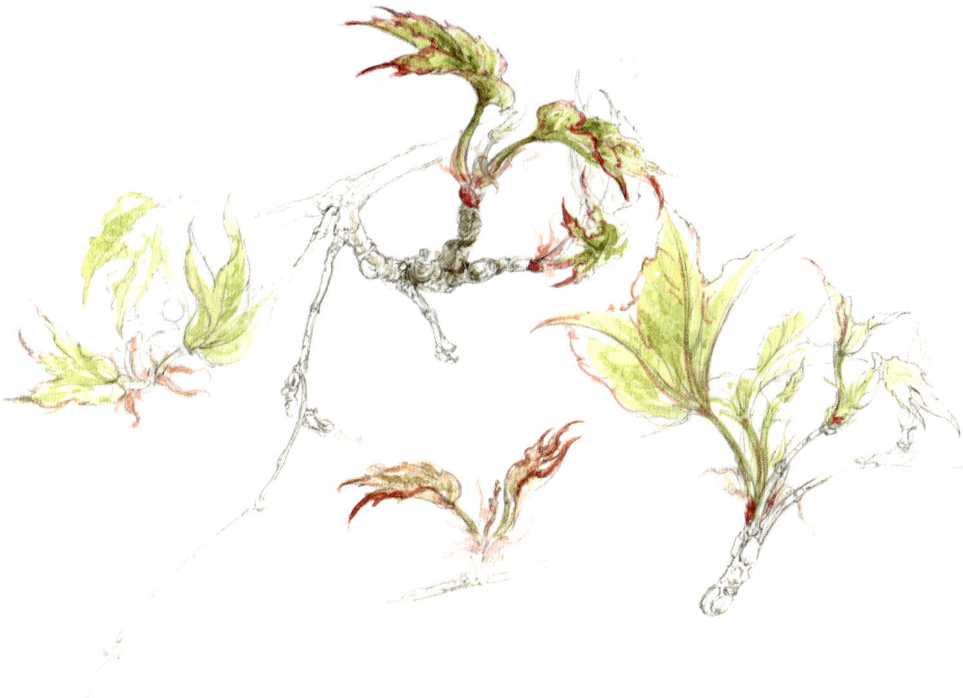

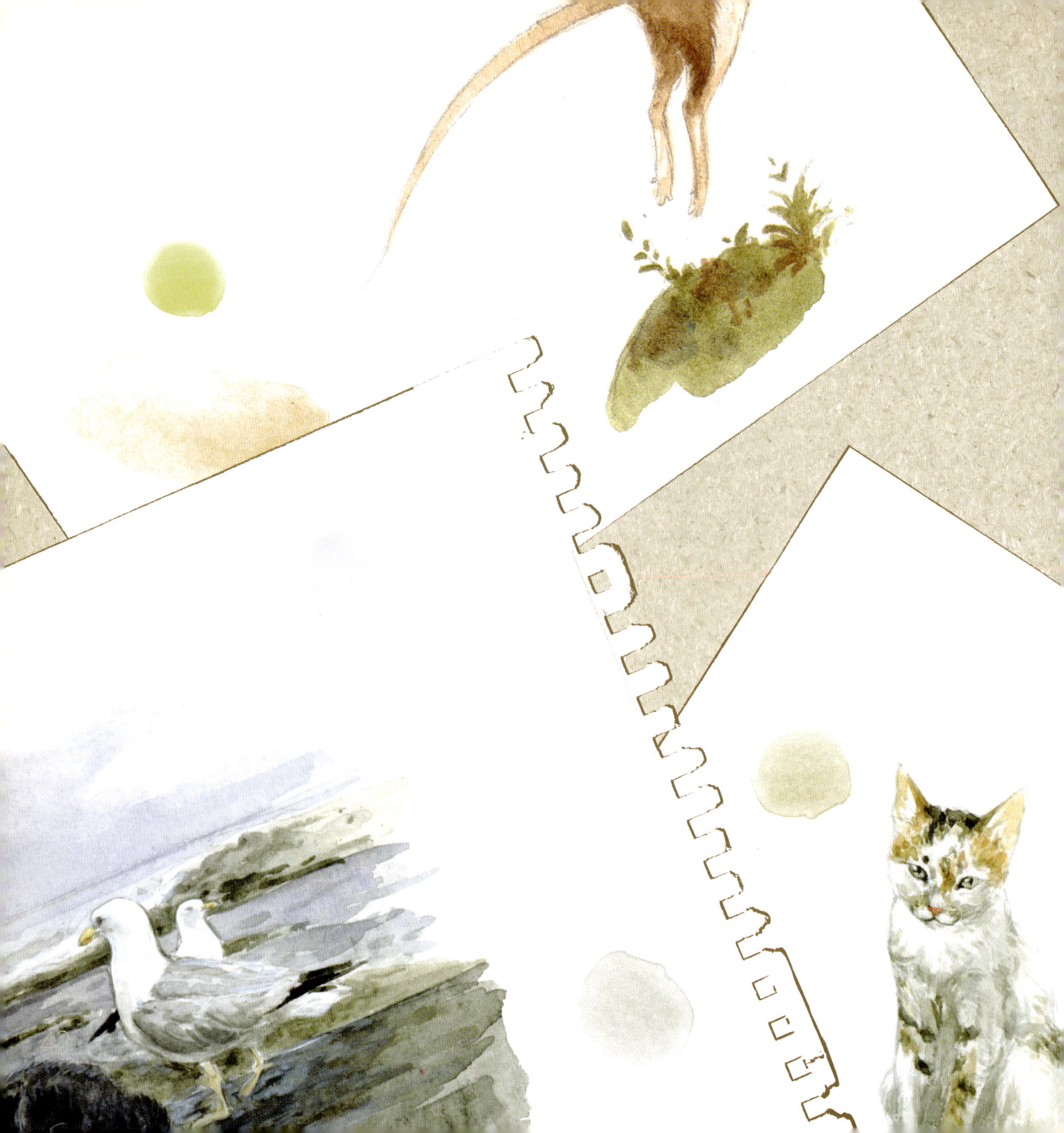

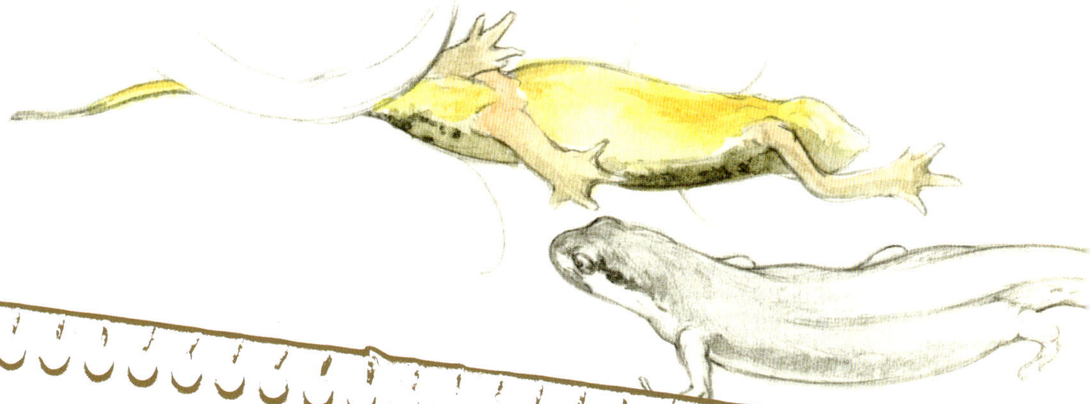

Encounters around the Corner

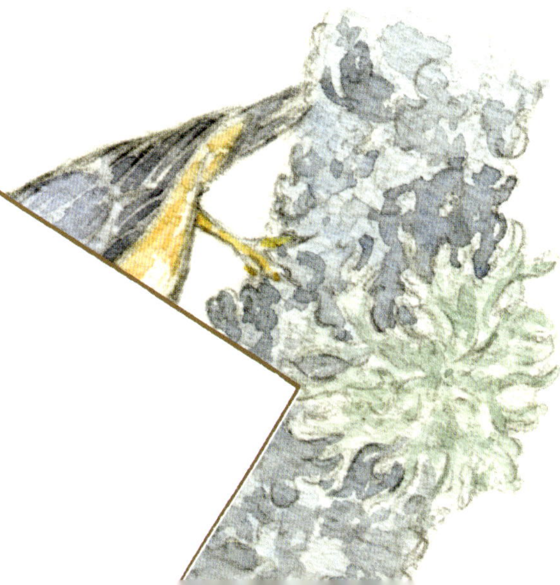

WHITE CAT

Cats are an inexhaustible subject for sketches and other studies. The whiteness of the cat's fur in this example is achieved by reserving the white of the paper in numerous spots, a key principle of watercolor.

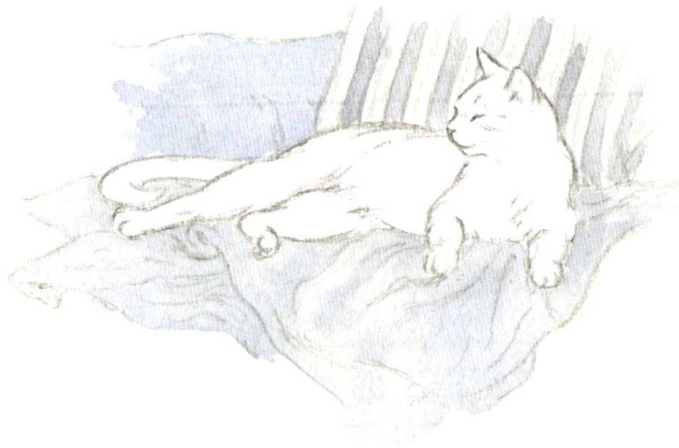

Colors:

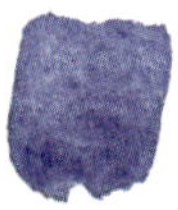

Ultramarine Blue

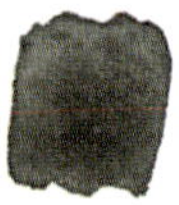

Payne's Gray

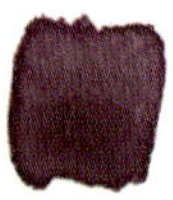

Permanent Mauve

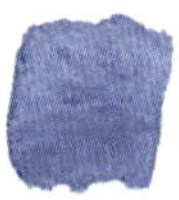

Cerulean Blue

1. Cover the blanket with a light wash of Ultramarine Blue, Payne's Gray, and a touch of Mauve. Apply a wash of Ultramarine Blue and Cerulean Blue to the cushion in the background. Do the same on the stripes with a mixture of Mauve, Ultramarine Blue, and Payne's Gray.

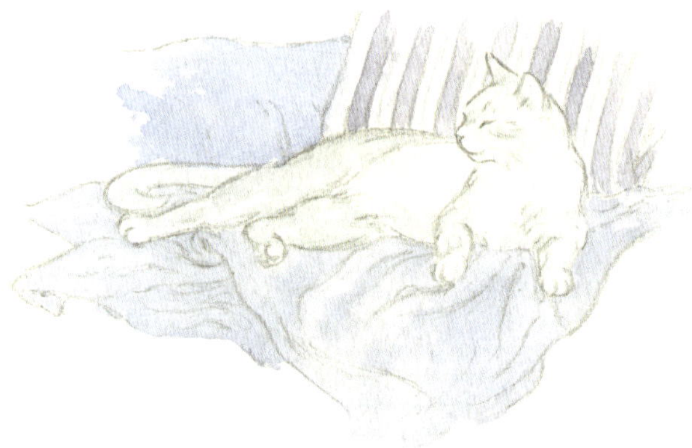

2. Apply a very light wash of Payne's Gray on the body of the cat in order to emphasize the relief, making sure to reserve the white of the paper in spots.

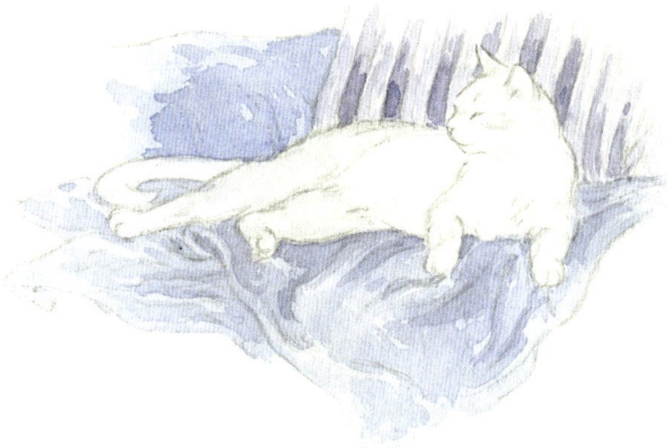

3. Accentuate the dimension of the fabric using more concentrated washes of the same mixtures as before.

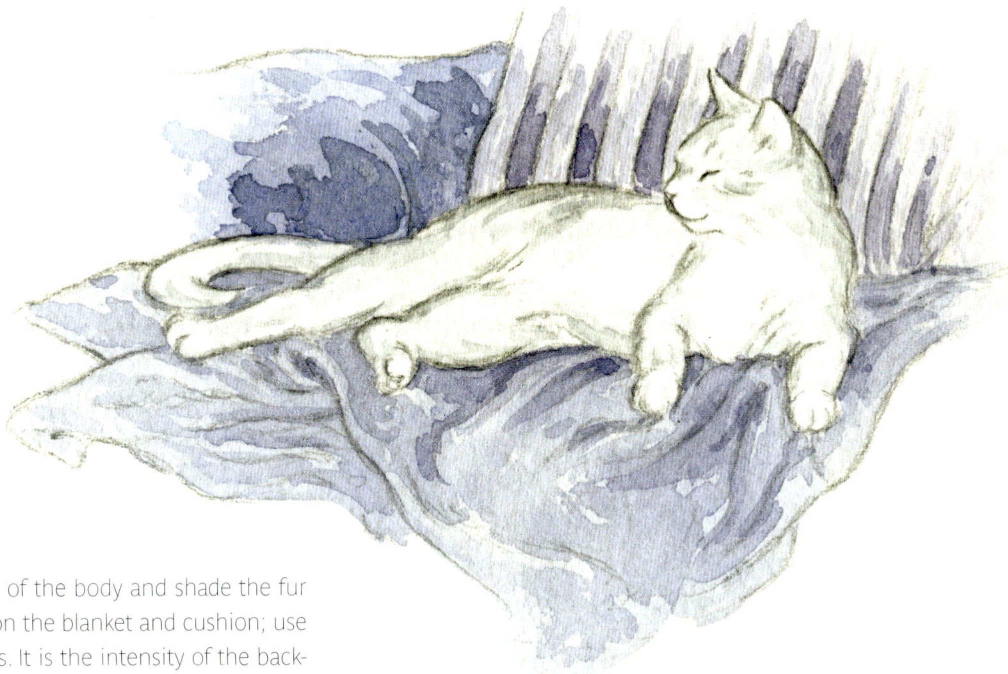

4. Using a fine brush, heighten the contours of the body and shade the fur with a wash of Payne's Gray. Apply a final wash on the blanket and cushion; use delicate touches of the more concentrated hues. It is the intensity of the background that makes the silhouette of the cat stand out.

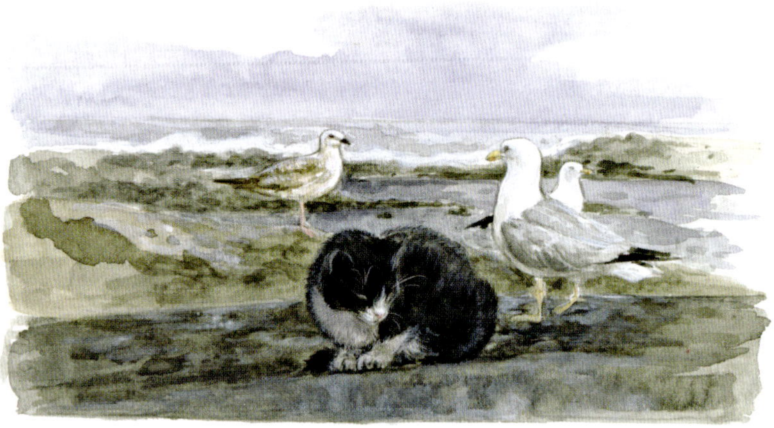

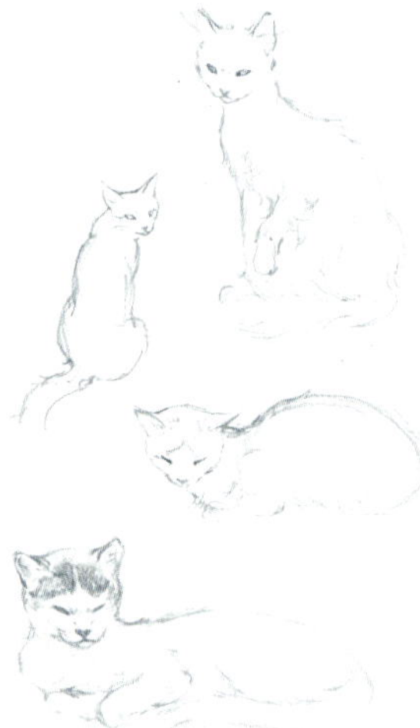

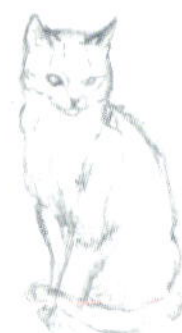

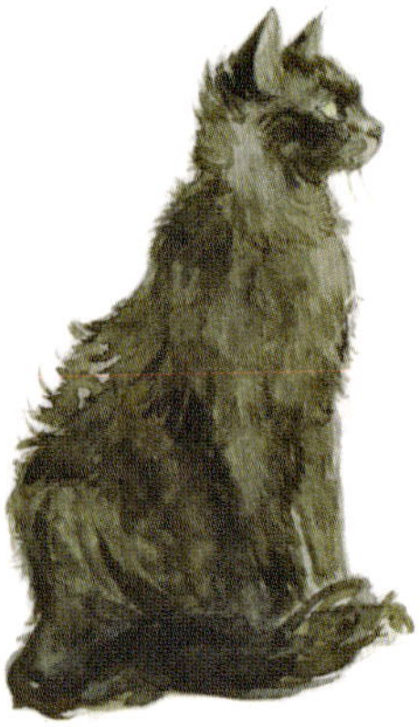

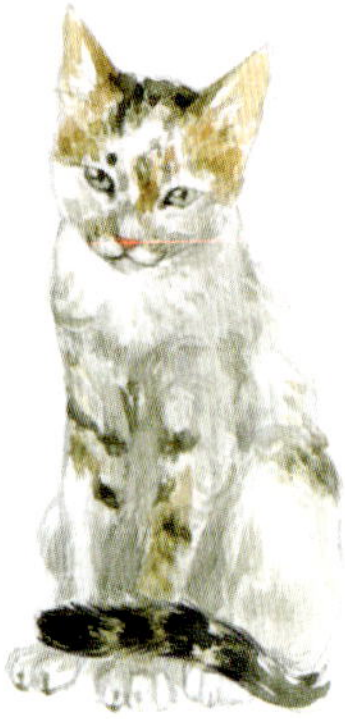

Cats

In painting cats, anything goes: working in wet-on-dry to reproduce the dimension of the fur, gestural brushstrokes, and abundant reserves of white to give the picture dynamism. No technique is inherently better for depicting a particular subject. Rather, you are faced with an essential question: "What do I want to highlight?" Choose your technique based on your answer.

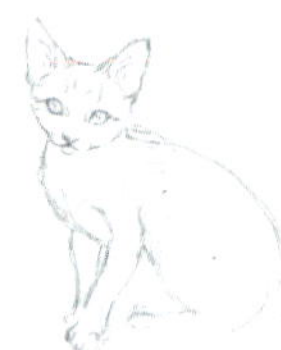

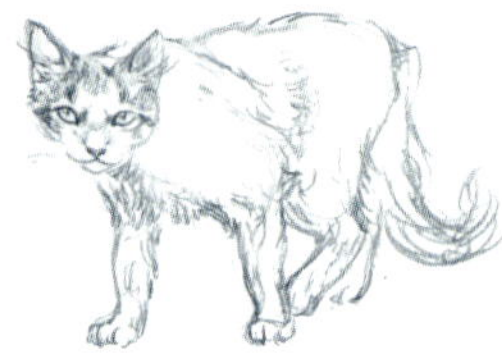

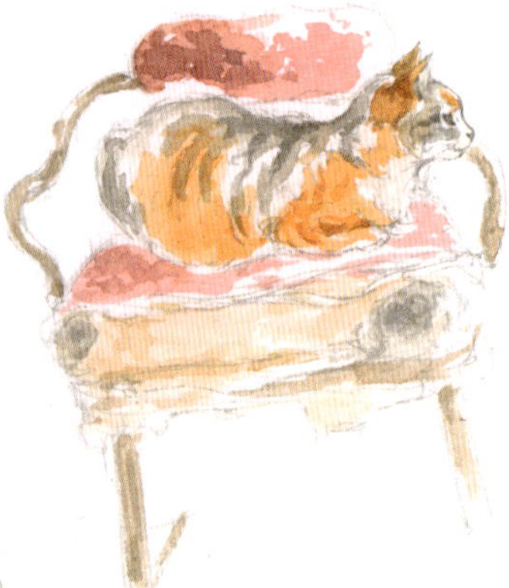

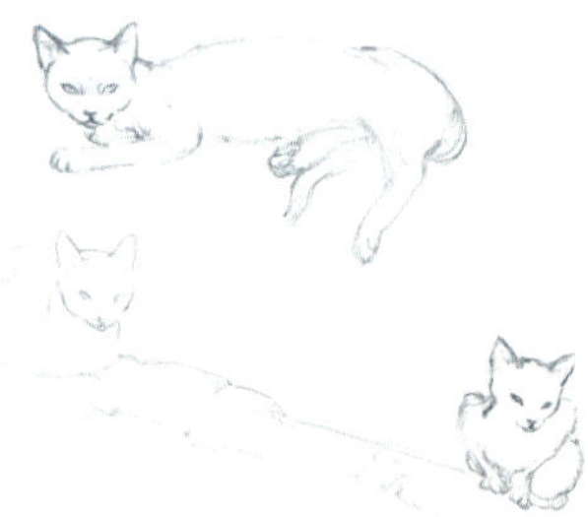

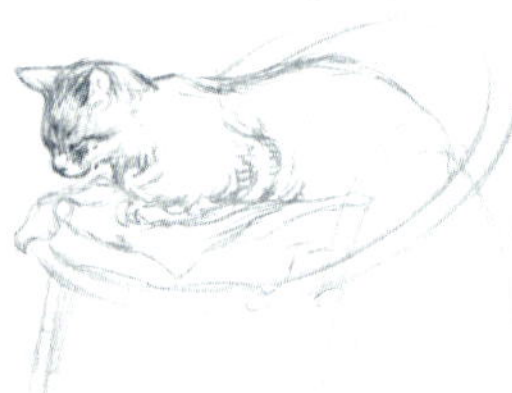

RED SQUIRREL ON A STUMP

In order to suggest the dynamism of the animal, I've posed it as though it's about to leap. Sketch and apply colors lightly so as not to freeze the movement.

Colors:

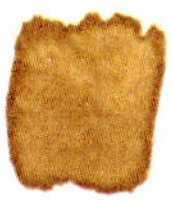
Burnt Sienna

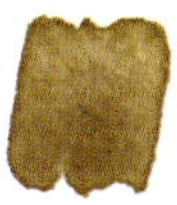
Burnt Umber

Cadmium Yellow Light

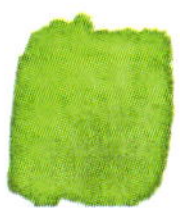
Sap Green

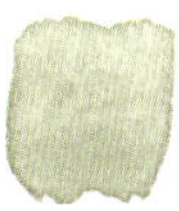
Davy's Gray

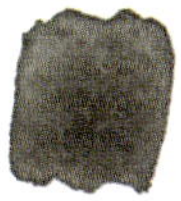
Payne's Gray

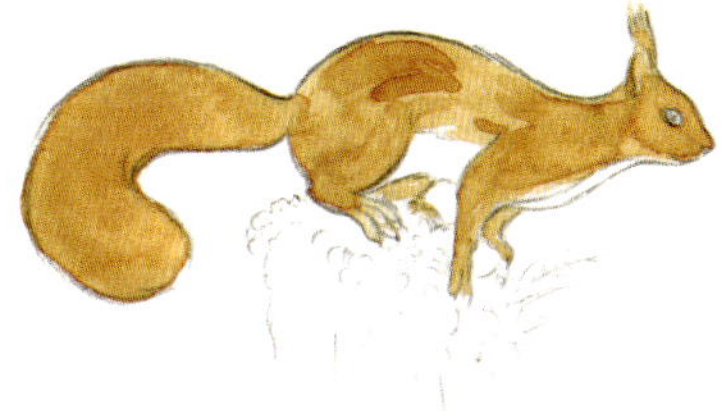

1. Apply an initial wash on the fur using a mixture of Burnt Sienna, Cadmium Yellow Light, and Burnt Umber.

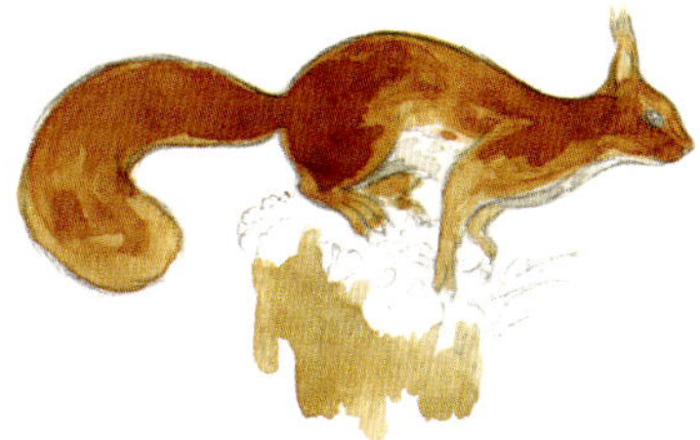

2. Working in wet-on-wet, emphasize certain areas of the fur with a more concentrated wash of this same mixture. Respect the direction of the fur. Shade the belly with a mix of the two grays. Apply a mix of Burnt Umber and Payne's Gray to the bark.

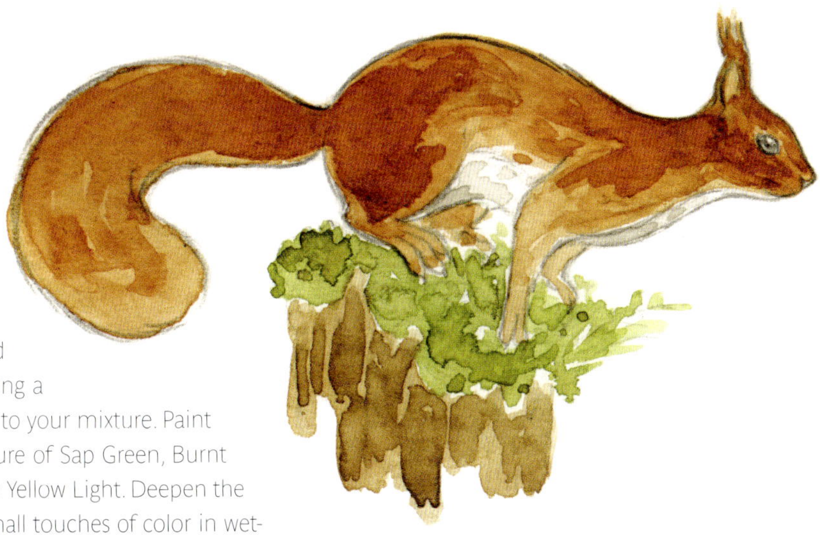

3. Apply a second wash to the bark, adding a bit more Payne's Gray to your mixture. Paint the moss with a mixture of Sap Green, Burnt Umber, and Cadmium Yellow Light. Deepen the tones in spots with small touches of color in wet-on-wet.

MARE AND FOAL

This duo demonstrates the technique of layering washes in order to show volume by deepening hues.

Colors:

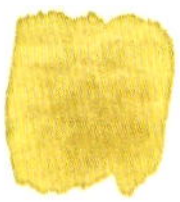

Yellow Ochre

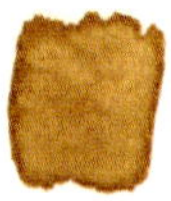

Burnt Sienna

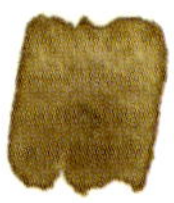

Burnt Umber

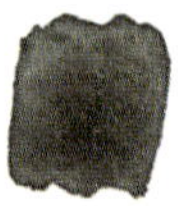

Payne's Gray

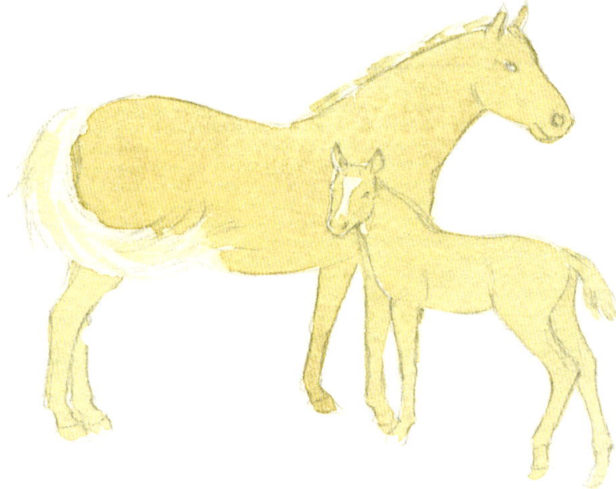

1. Moisten the drawing except for the mare's tail and mane, and the white mark on the foal's face. Apply a mixture of Yellow Ochre, Burnt Sienna, and Burnt Umber.

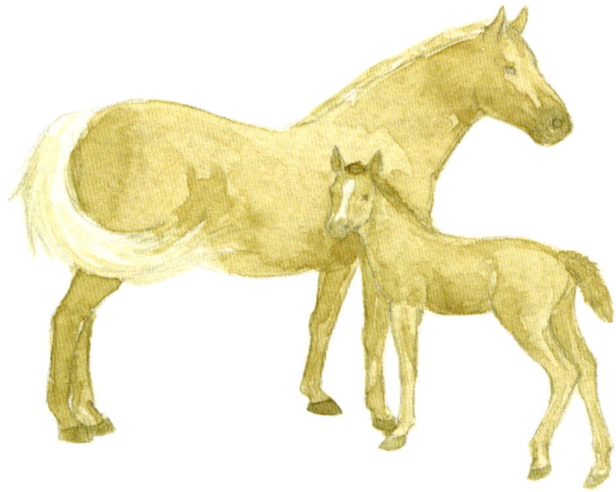

2. Create volume using a second, more concentrated wash in wet-on-wet. Add a touch of Payne's Gray to the mixture for the hooves and muzzles.

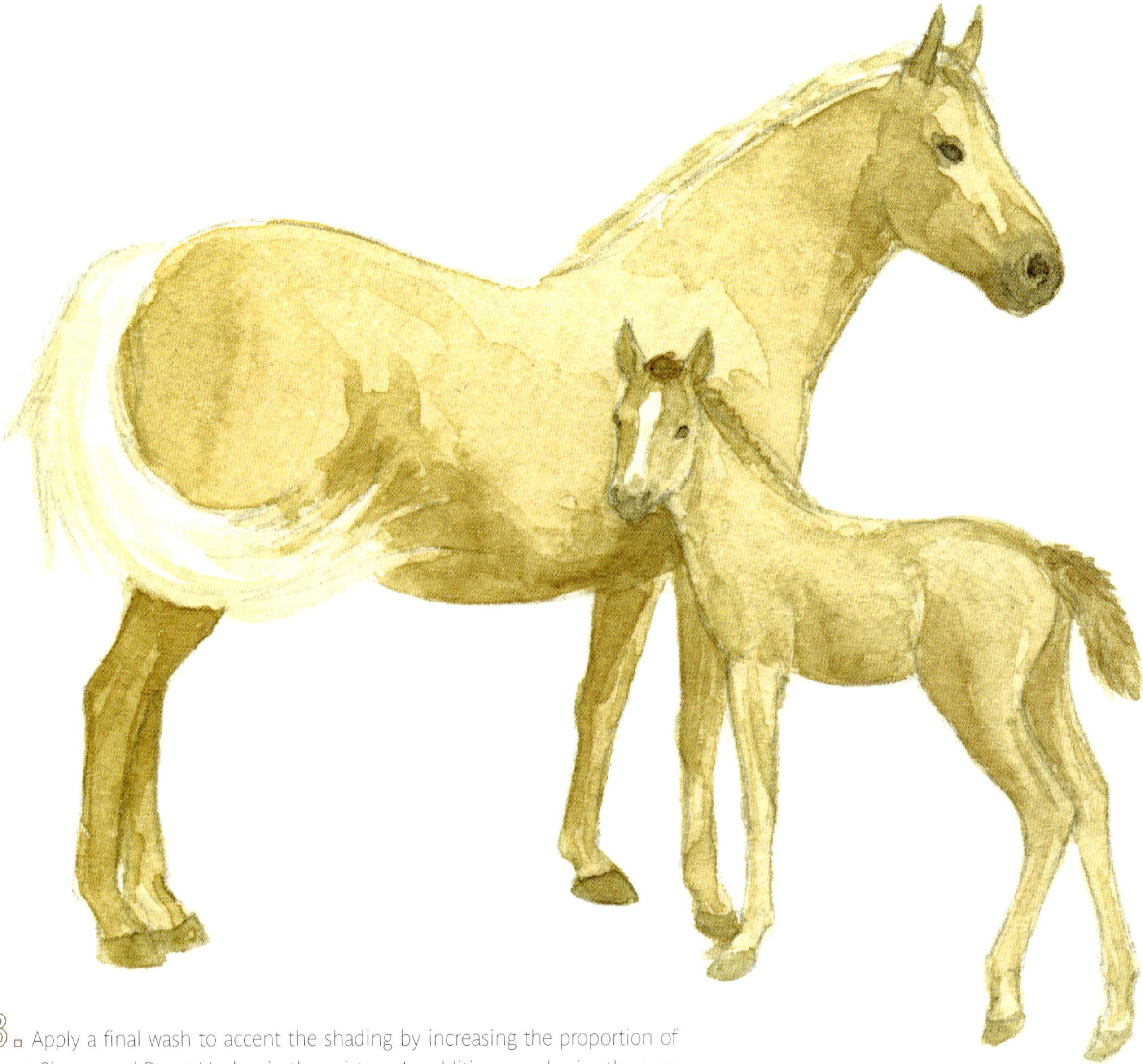

3. Apply a final wash to accent the shading by increasing the proportion of Burnt Sienna and Burnt Umber in the mixture. In addition, emphasize the eyes and nostrils by adding a bit of Payne's Gray to them.

HORSE AGAINST A STORMY SKY

The fields in which horses graze often offer little visual interest. However, by focusing on the harmony and juxtaposition of colors, you can still depict a setting that enhances your subject.

Colors:

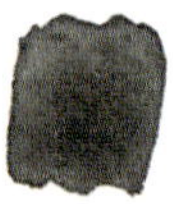
Payne's Gray

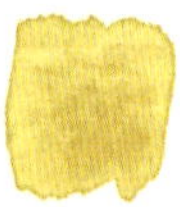
Yellow Ochre

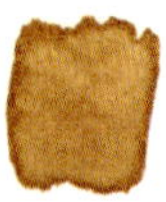
Burnt Sienna

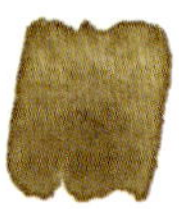
Burnt Umber

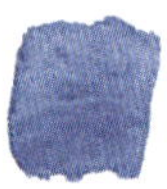
Cerulean Blue

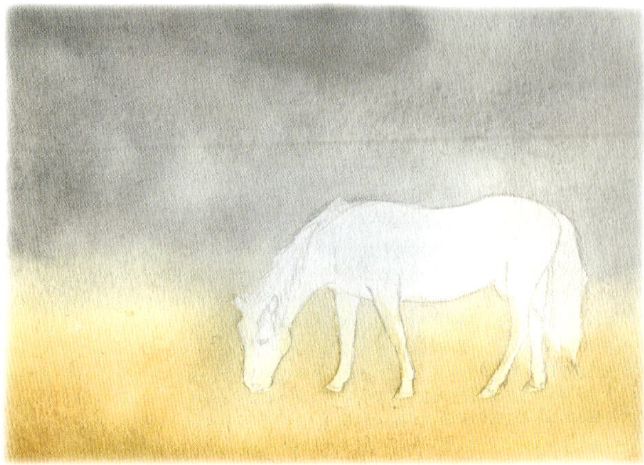

1. Moisten the background generously, then apply a wash of Payne's Gray to the sky and a mixture of Yellow Ochre, Burnt Sienna, and Burnt Umber to the ground. Let the two colors blend where they meet, then soak up the excess with a dry brush.

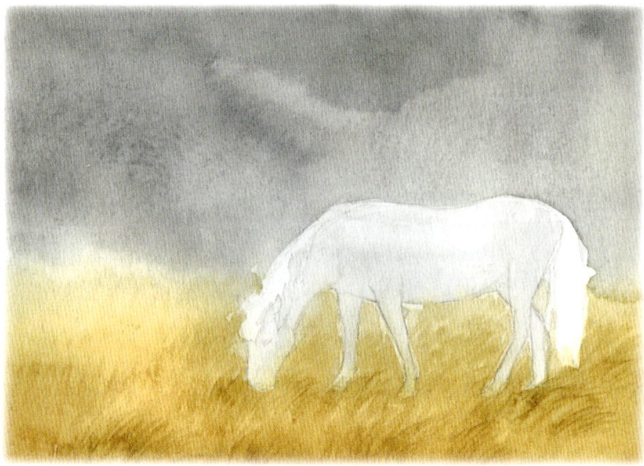

2. Apply a very diluted wash of Payne's Gray with a touch of Cerulean Blue to the body of the horse, leaving the mane and tail white. Re-moisten the background and heighten the colors of the sky and grass with another more intense wash. Using a dry brush, create relief in the dry grass by brushing the ground with short angled strokes.

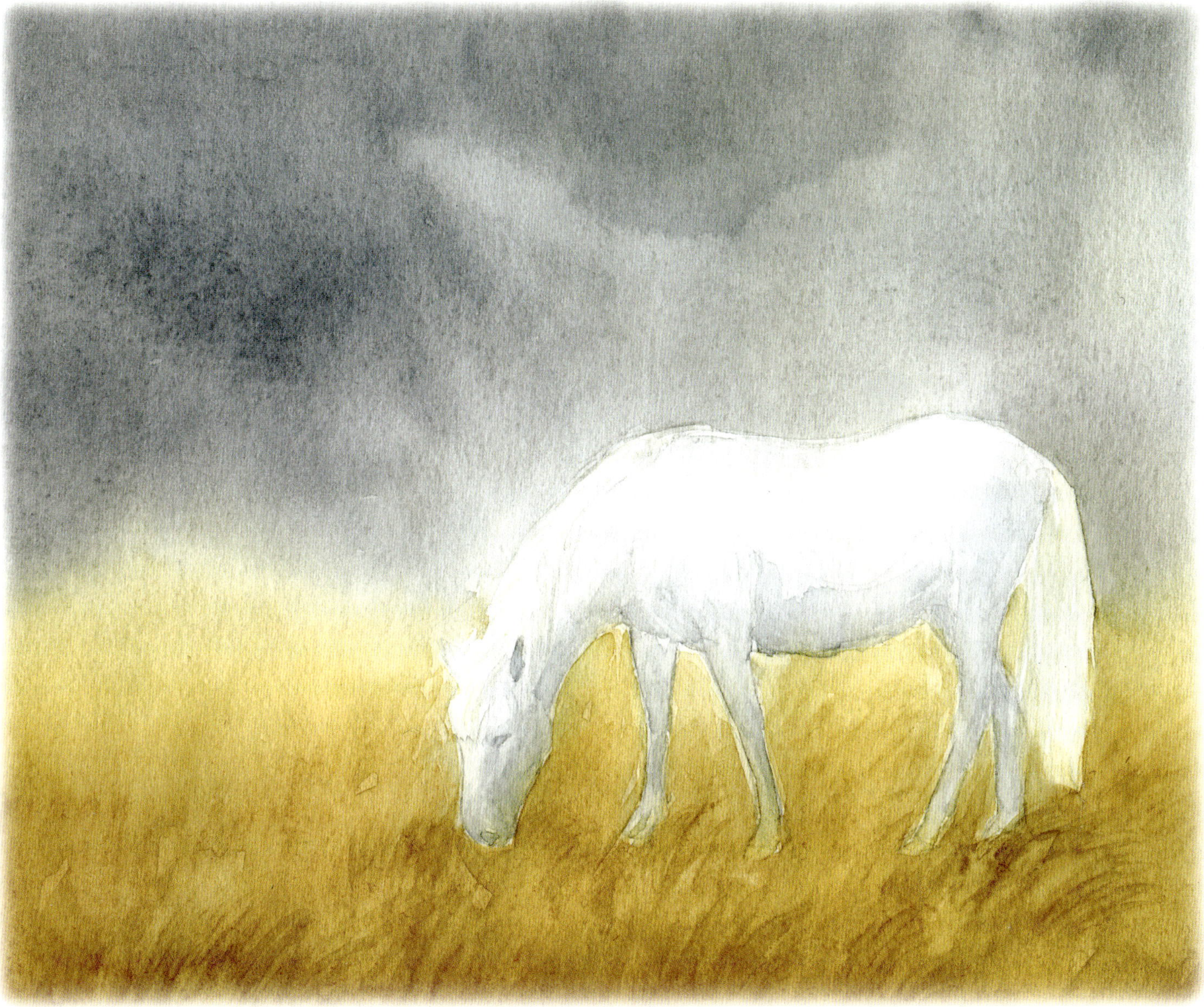

3. Apply a very diluted mixture of Yellow Ochre and Burnt Umber with a touch of Payne's Gray to the tail and mane. Give them some added dimension with a wash of Payne's Gray and Cerulean Blue. Accentuate the sky and the grass with a final wash.

SWALLOW

Graceful and slender as the tip of a brush, swallows perched on electric wires lend themselves to plein air sketching.

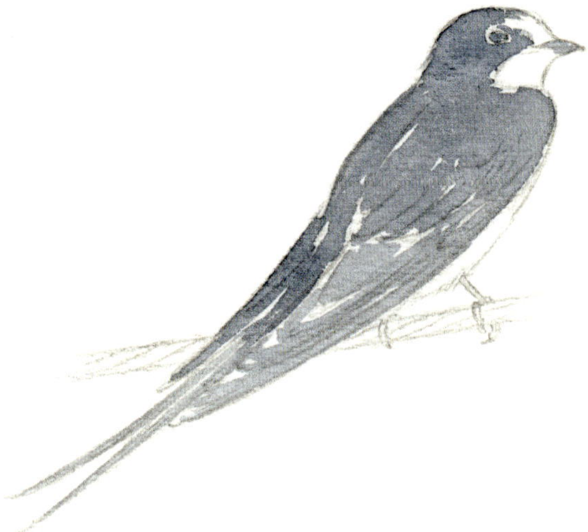

Colors:

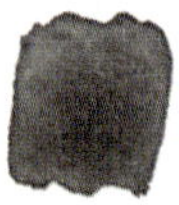 Payne's Gray

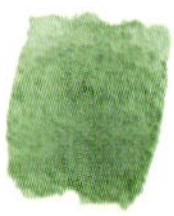 Emerald Green

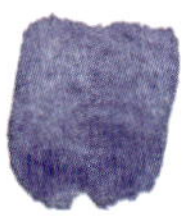 Ultramarine Blue

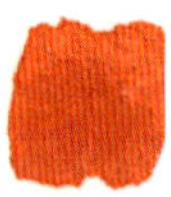 Cadmium Red Deep

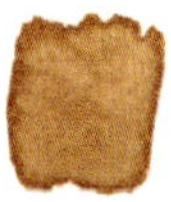 Burnt Sienna

1. Apply a diluted wash of Payne's Gray, Emerald Green, and Ultramarine Blue to your sketch. This tinted gray will do justice to the sparkling luminosity of the plumage. Reserve a few white spots on the head and belly, between some of the feathers, and around the eye in order to bring some light and roundness to the body.

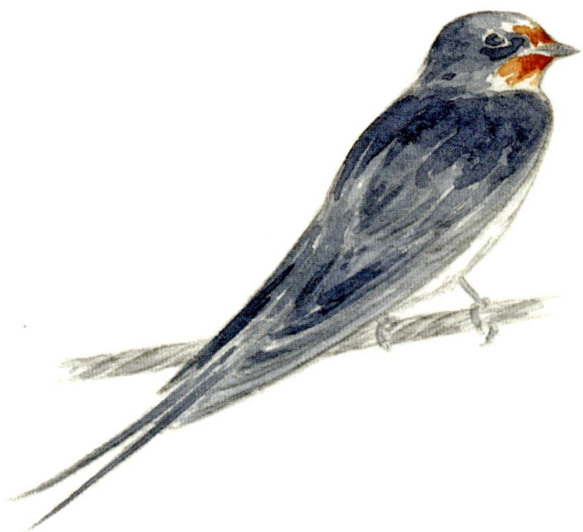

2. Apply the same mixture in a second, denser wash on certain sections: the back of the head, the top of the back, and then, using delicate brushstrokes, along the sketched lines of the feathers. Paint the claws and the wire with a wash of Payne's Gray, and add a touch of Cadmium Red Deep and Burnt Sienna to the head.

EUROPEAN GOLDFINCH

This small songbird has brilliant colors that highly concentrated pigments will render precisely.

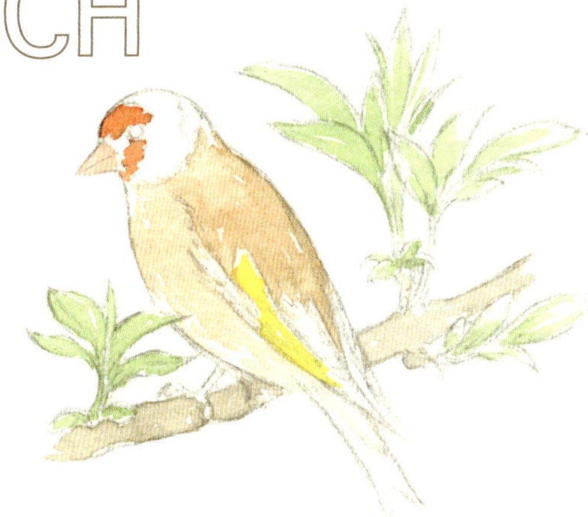

Colors:

Rose Madder

Yellow Ochre

Burnt Umber

Ultramarine Blue

Cadmium Red Deep

Payne's Gray

Cadmium Yellow Deep

Raw Umber

Sap Green

1. Apply a wash of Rose Madder and Burnt Umber to the body of the bird, reserving the white of the paper in spots. Place a few touches of Cadmium Red Deep and Rose Madder on the head as well as a stroke of Cadmium Yellow Deep on the wing. Apply a mixture of Raw Umber and Burnt Umber on the branch, and a wash of Sap Green, Yellow Ochre, and Ultramarine Blue on the leaves.

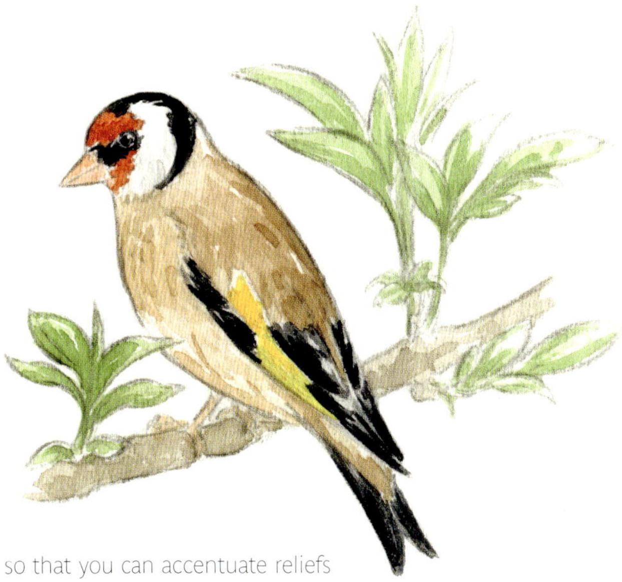

2. Keep these mixtures so that you can accentuate reliefs with denser washes in small strokes. Lightly shade the white part of the head with a very diluted wash of Payne's Gray. Finally, to give structure and depth to the painted bird, add the black areas of the plumage by applying a mixture of Payne's Gray and Burnt Umber with a fine brush.

NUTHATCH

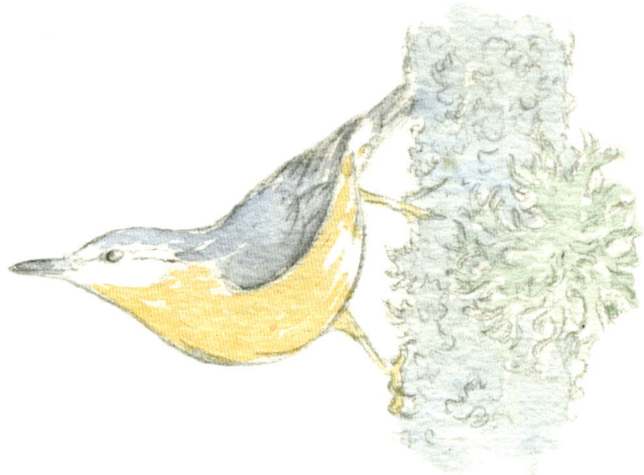

This acrobat can hop around a tree trunk upside down. The color of the lichen surrounding it highlights the color of its plumage.

1. Apply a wash of Indian Yellow and Burnt Sienna on the belly and claws; on the back, a mixture of Ultramarine Blue, Payne's Gray, and Cerulean Blue. Paint the trunk with a mixture of Cerulean Blue and Payne's Gray. Apply a wash of Emerald Green and Payne's Gray to the tuft of lichen.

Colors:

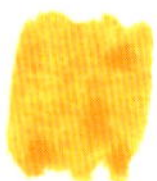 Indian Yellow

 Emerald Green

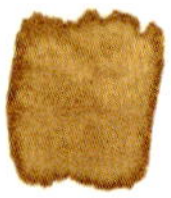 Burnt Sienna

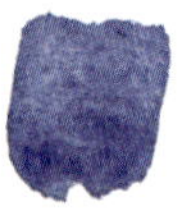 Ultramarine Blue

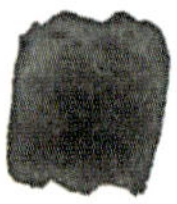 Payne's Gray

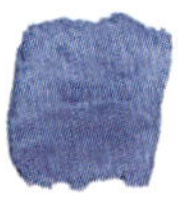 Cerulean Blue

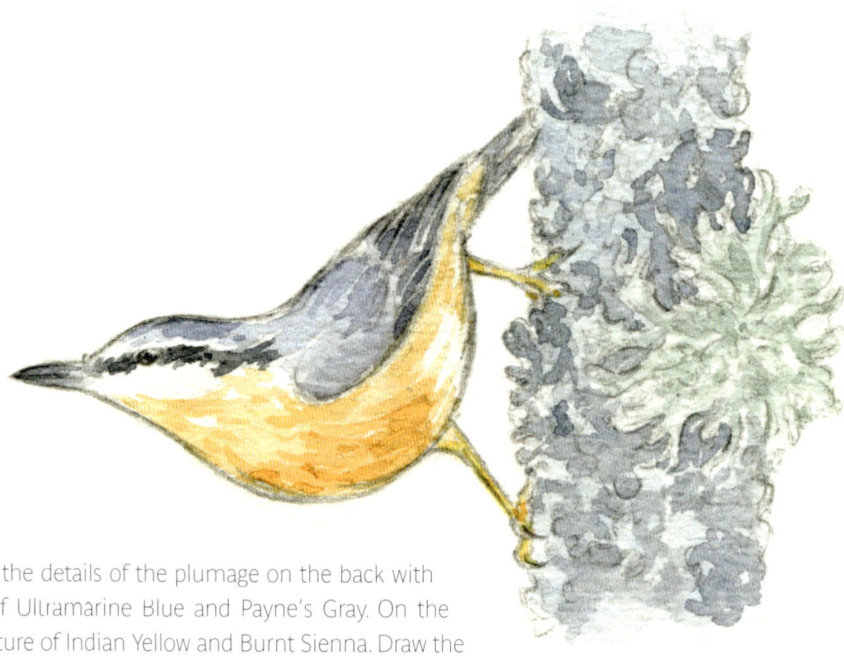

2. Bring out the details of the plumage on the back with small strokes of Ultramarine Blue and Payne's Gray. On the belly, use a mixture of Indian Yellow and Burnt Sienna. Draw the dark "mask," the eye, and the beak of the bird with a wash of Payne's Gray. Give the lichen extra density with a second, deeper-colored wash.

Small Animals

Let the surprises you find on your walks dictate how each page is organized in your watercolor sketchbooks. Don't try to create a scale based on the size of the first image you paint. The space you have available determines the scale of each new sketch or painting, which is in itself an educational exercise: it's up to you to adapt your watercolor to the format.

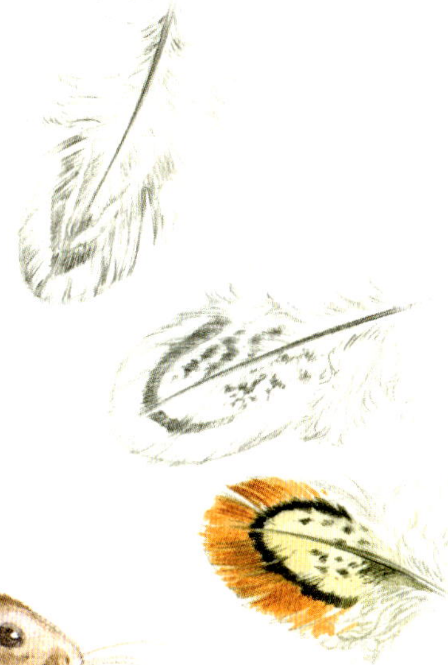

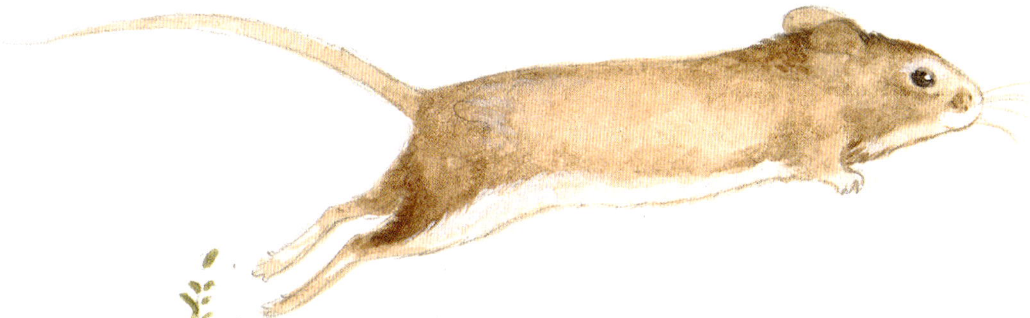

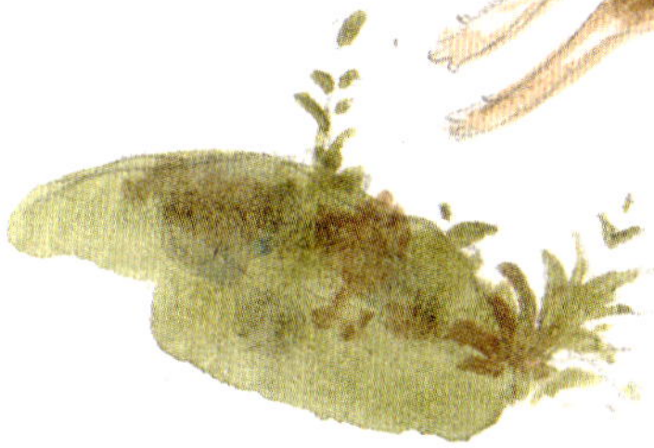

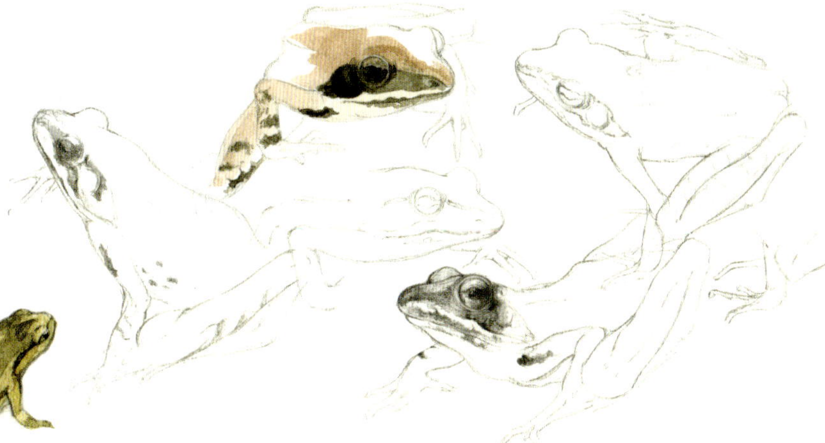

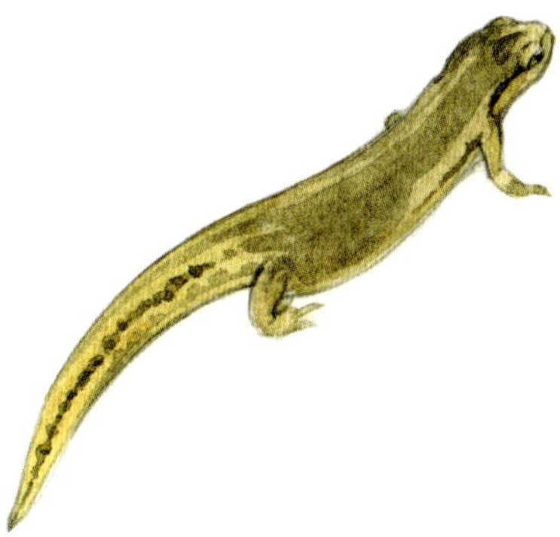

GARDEN BLUE TIT

Some brave passerine birds allow themselves to be sketched. This is true of blue tits and chickadees, regulars in barns and gardens.

Colors:

- Cadmium Yellow Lemon
- Indian Yellow
- Ultramarine Blue
- Cerulean Blue
- Payne's Gray
- Terre Verte
- Sap Green
- Green Gold

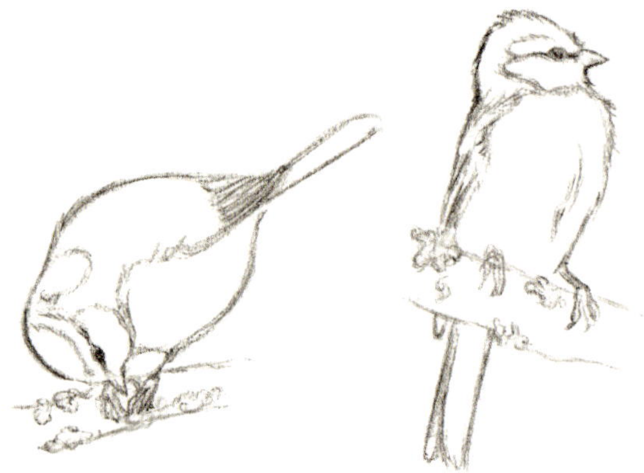

1. Make quick sketches with an HB pencil. Try to capture dynamic postures.

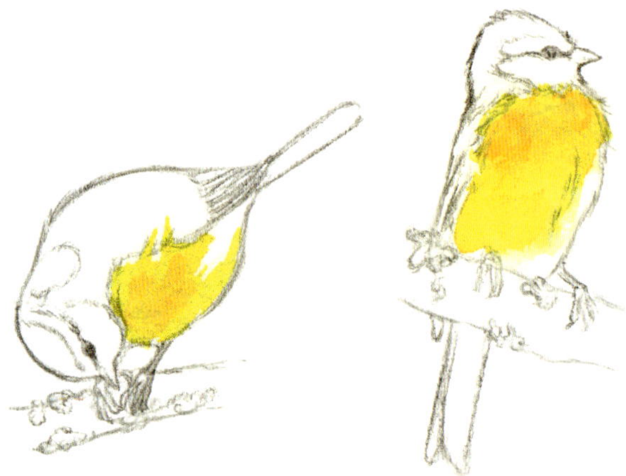

2. Using a wash brush, place a large splash of Cadmium Yellow Lemon on the breast. On the wet color add a dash of Indian Yellow around the throat.

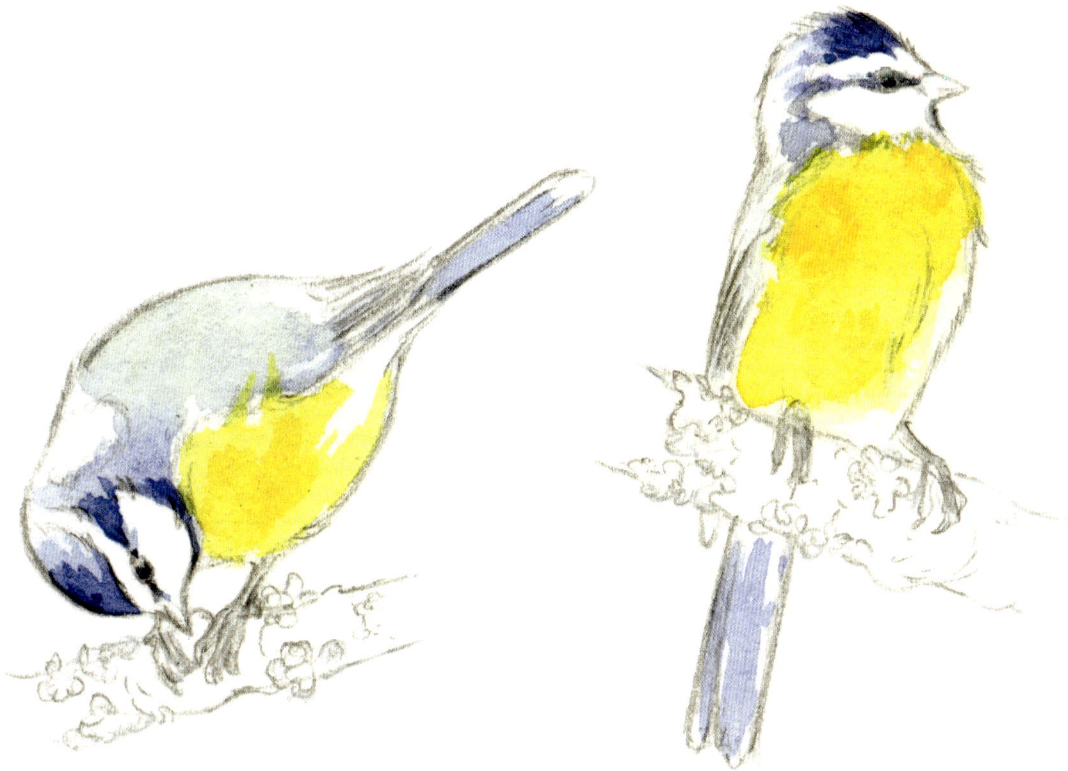

3. Apply a diluted mixture of Ultramarine Blue Deep and Cerulean Blue to the feathers, using a fine brush and delicate, small strokes; make sure to brush in the direction of the feathers, from front to back. Lightly moisten the back of the bent-over bird. Add a touch of Cadmium Yellow Lemon to the preceding mixture and apply with a medium brush. Using the fine brush and diluted Ultramarine Blue, lightly emphasize the intensity of the plumage on the head. Paint the contours and the interior of the eyes with slightly diluted Payne's Gray and a very fine brush. Leave a small white area in the interior of each eye to suggest a sparkle.

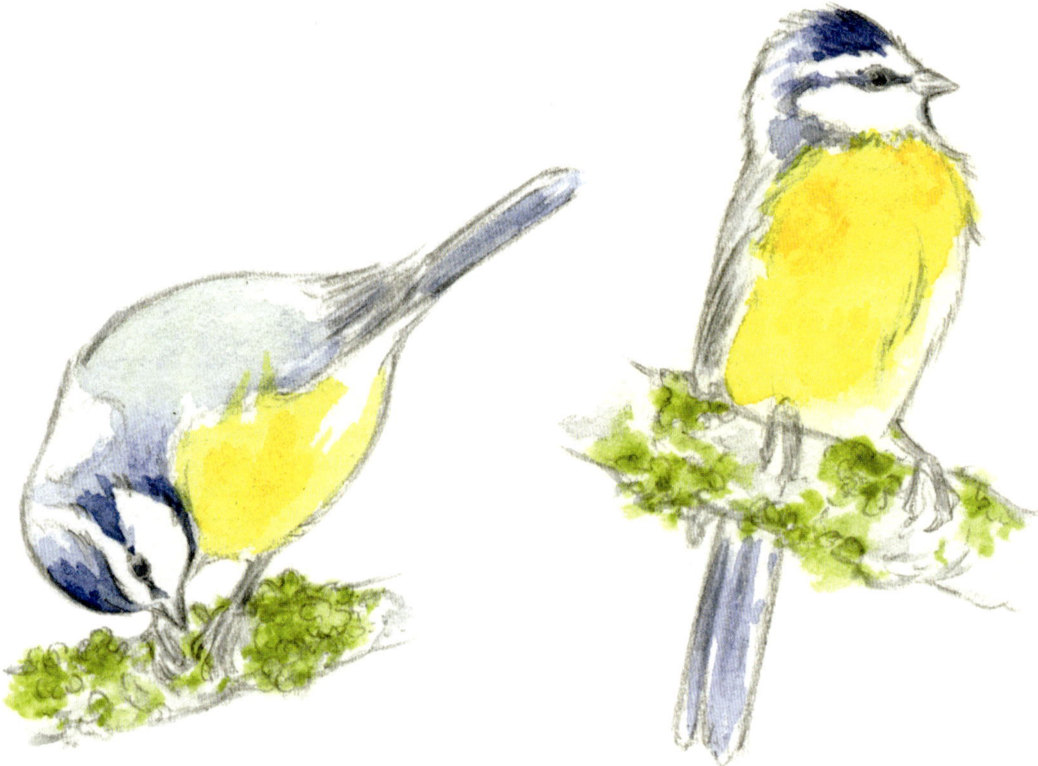

4. With an HB pencil, gently add weight to the things that need more emphasis —in this case, the drawing of the lichen-covered branch, the tails, and the claws. Finally, add a few touches of Terre Verte mixed with Sap Green on the lichen using a medium brush; on the still-wet paint add a few dashes of Green Gold.

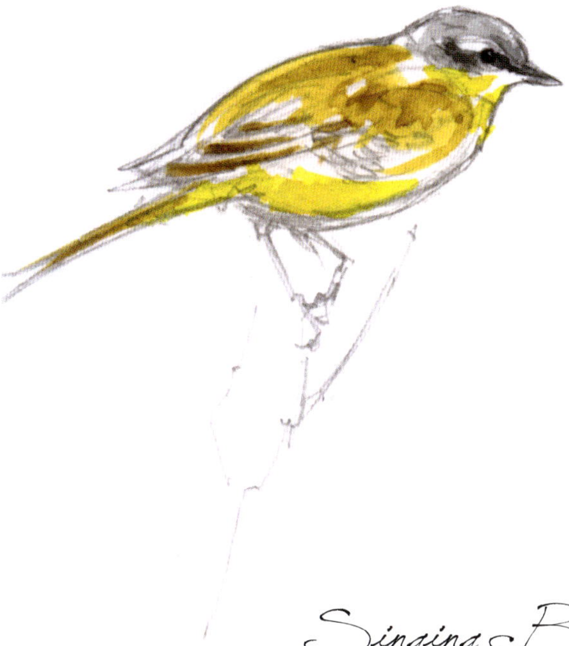

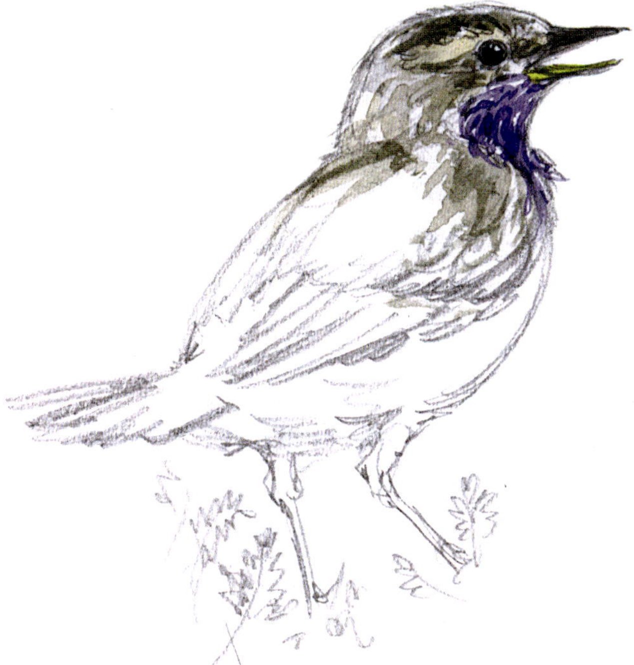

Singing Birds

Sketching birds from life can be a challenge. The speedy models often are hardly obliging, sometimes holding a pose for several moments only to take flight as soon as the watercolor box is opened! Pay close attention and remember key features. You can lightly sketch the contours and colors of plumage even if the pose has changed.

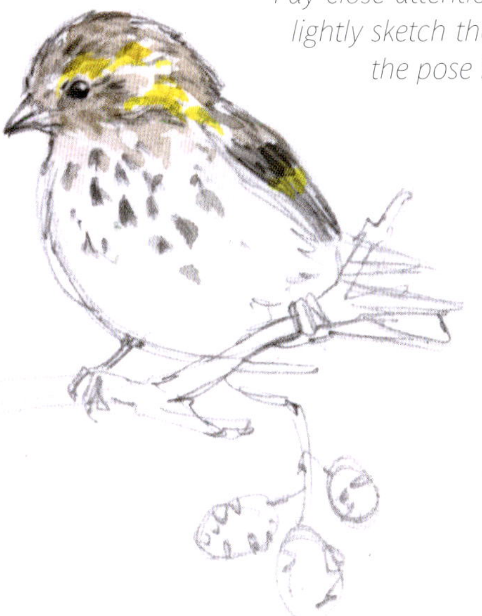

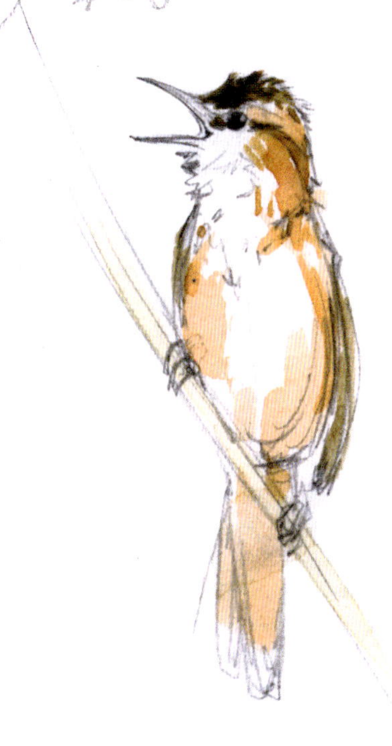

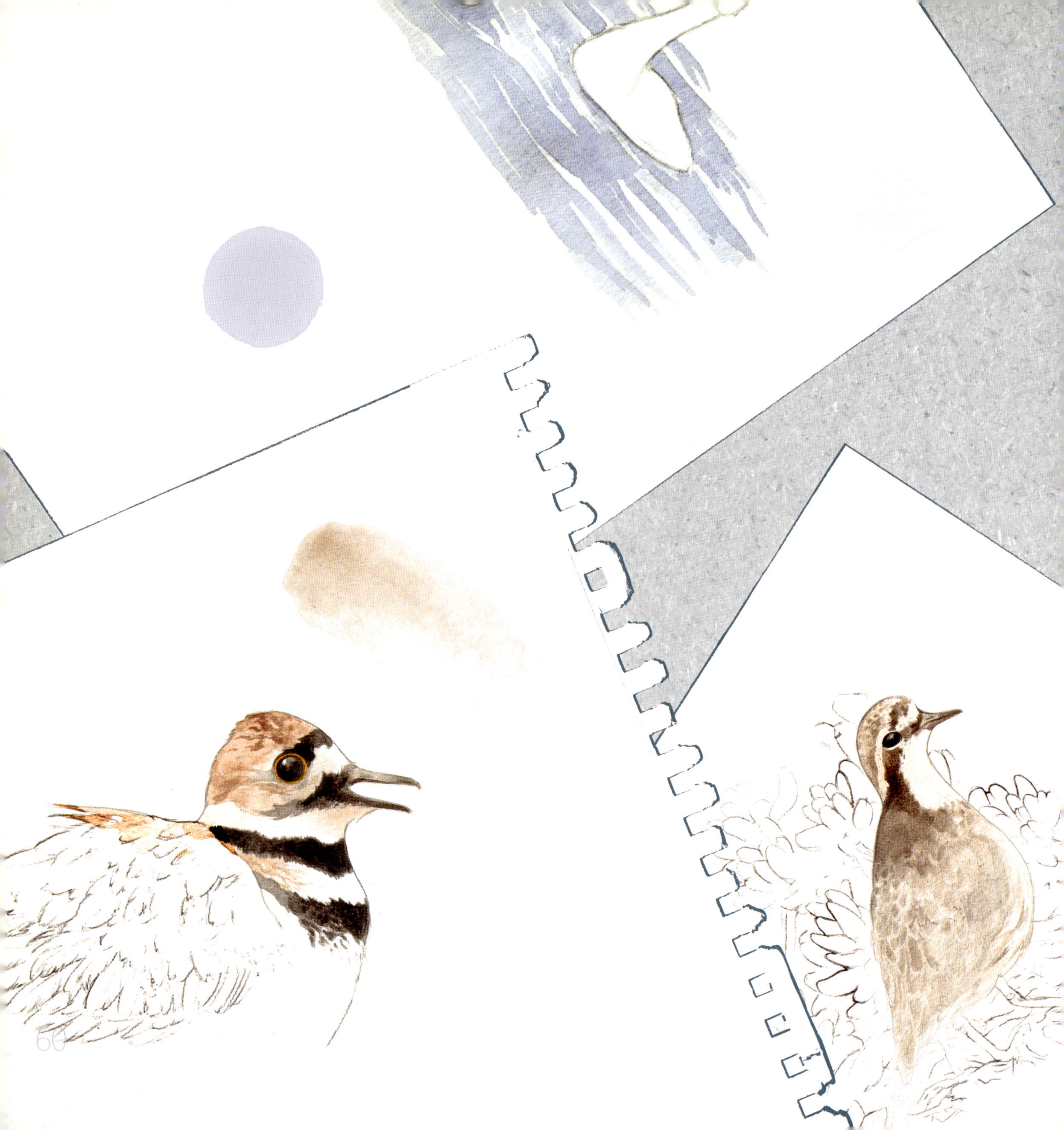

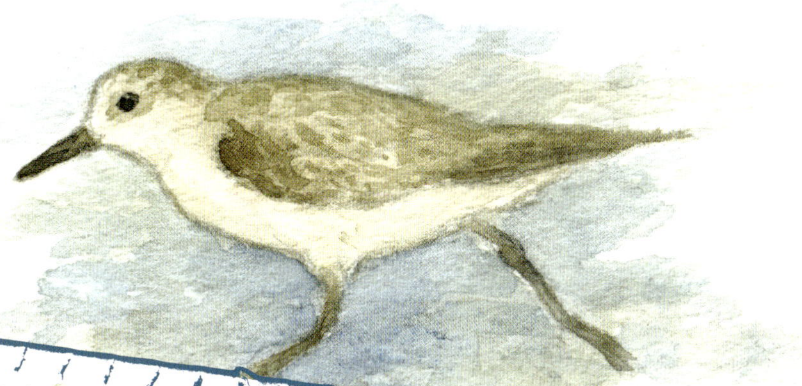

At the Water's Edge... and Beyond

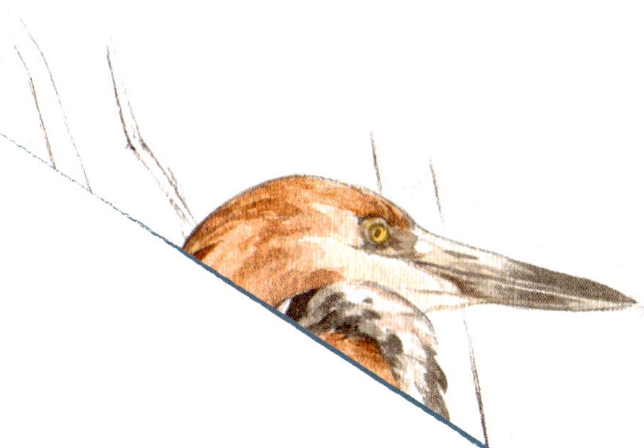

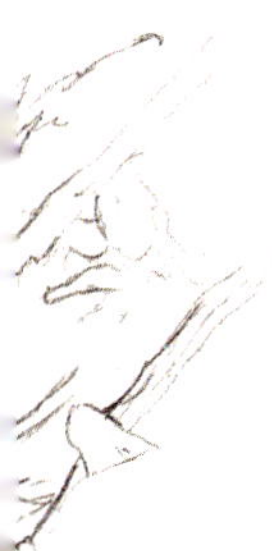

NESTING SEAGULL

This black-headed gull sitting in its nest could only be observed from a distance, using a telephoto lens, so that it would not be disturbed. The surrounding foliage works well to bring out the dark brown cap of its summer plumage.

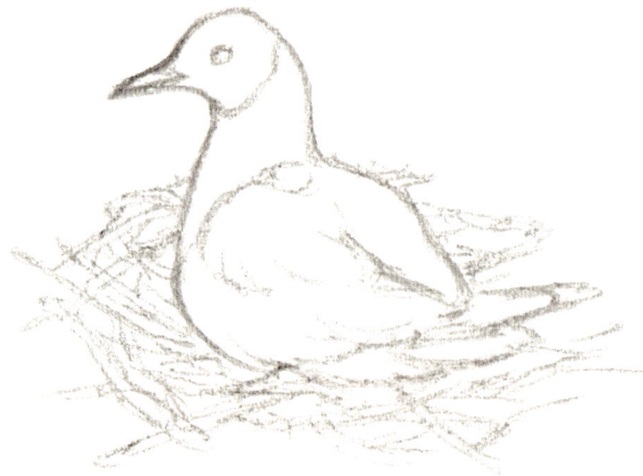

Colors:

Payne's Gray

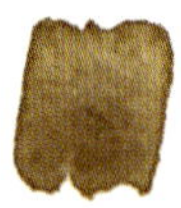

Burnt Umber

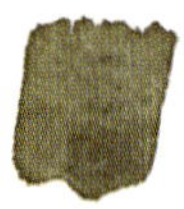

Sepia

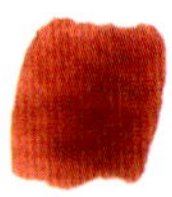

Alizarin Crimson

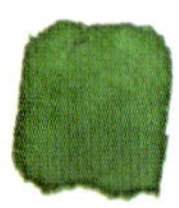

Hooker's Green

1. Rapidly sketch the general form of the bird, giving the body a simple, rounded shape.

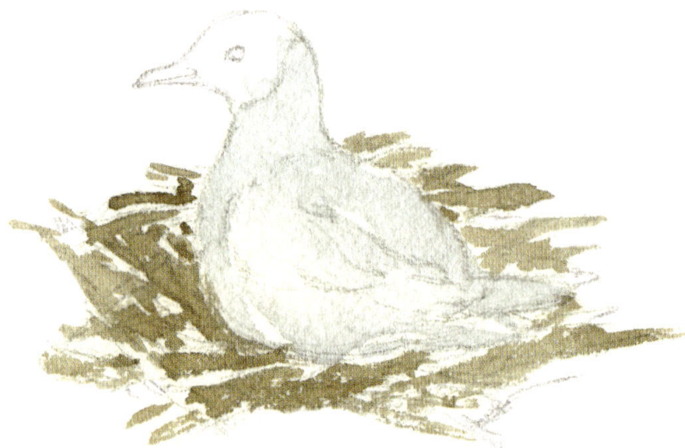

2. Apply a light wash of Payne's Gray on the body, then paint the most prominent twigs with a mixture of Burnt Umber and Payne's Gray. Don't use too much water, because you want to convey the twigs' roughness.

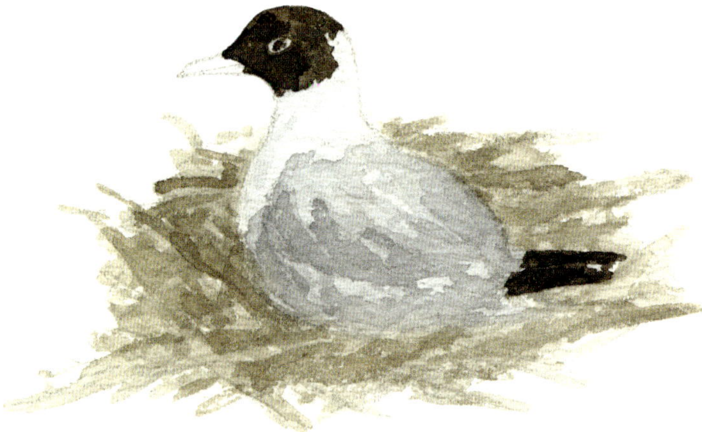

3. Using a mixture of Sepia and Payne's Gray, paint the black cap and tail. Reserve a bit of white in the eye; then shape the volume of the plumage with a wash of Payne's Gray. Apply a diluted wash of Burnt Umber and Payne's Gray on the nest, so that no more white remains but the twigs you painted in the last step are still visible.

4. Create a mixture of Alizarin Crimson and Payne's Gray for the beak. Use two washes to give it dimension. Accent the shading of the plumage with a wash of Payne's Gray.

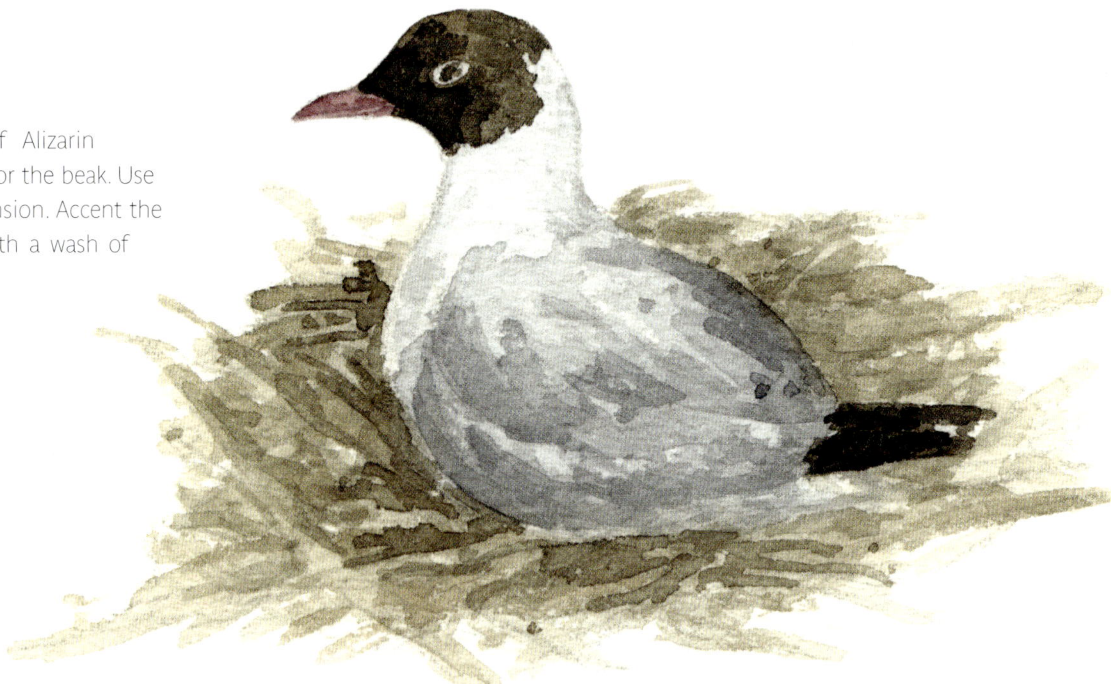

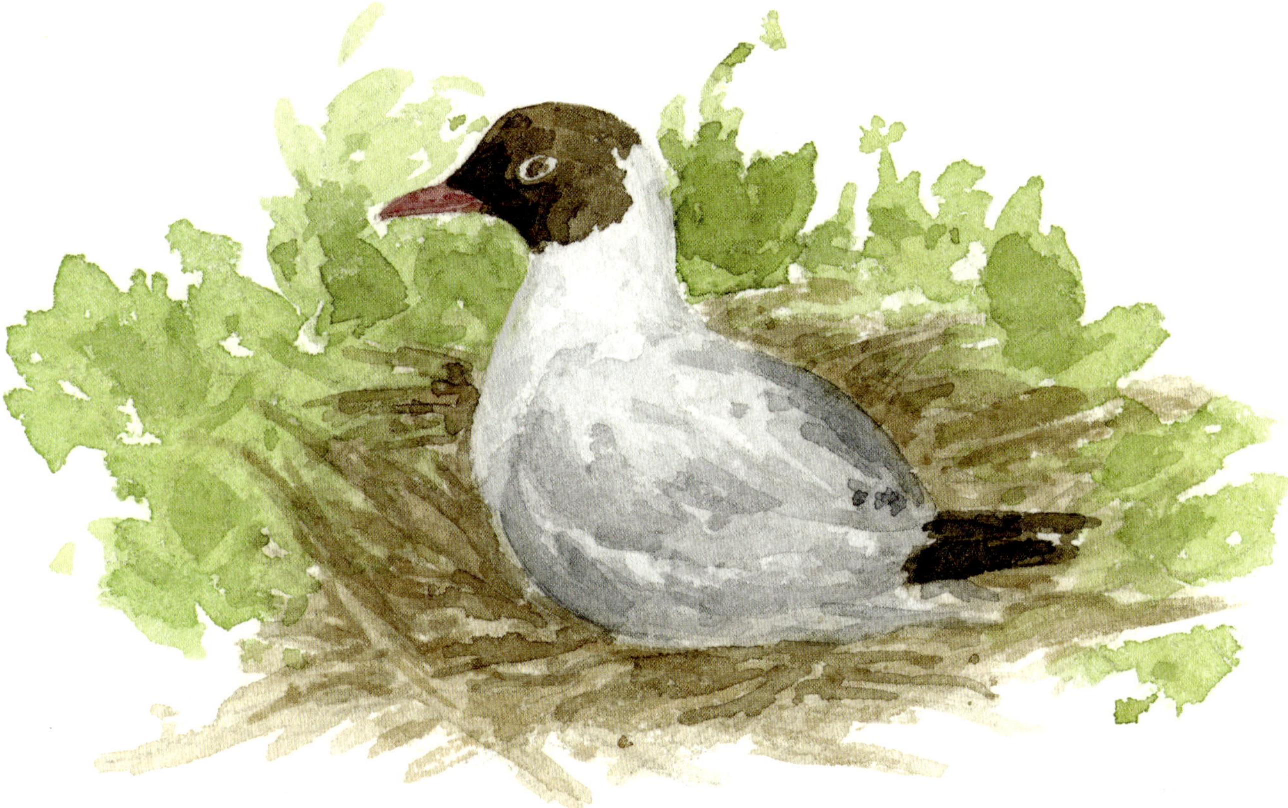

5. Using quick dynamic strokes, paint the foliage in the background with a wash of Hooker's Green and some Burnt Umber. Don't use too much detail, as you don't want to draw attention away from the main subject.

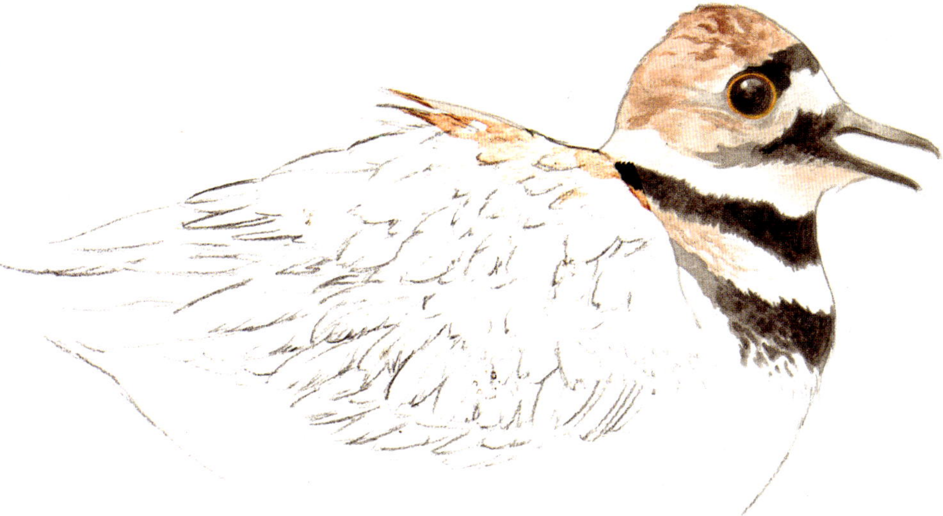

Aquatic Birds

In the same way you might paint the movement of a wave, your brushstrokes should follow the movement of the feathers. Observe the motion of the wading bird: the twisting of the neck is indicated by fine parallel brushstrokes that curve from the head and neck into the back. Beneath the washes, glimpses of white paper should appear like reflections of light on the plumage, giving it a silky appearance.

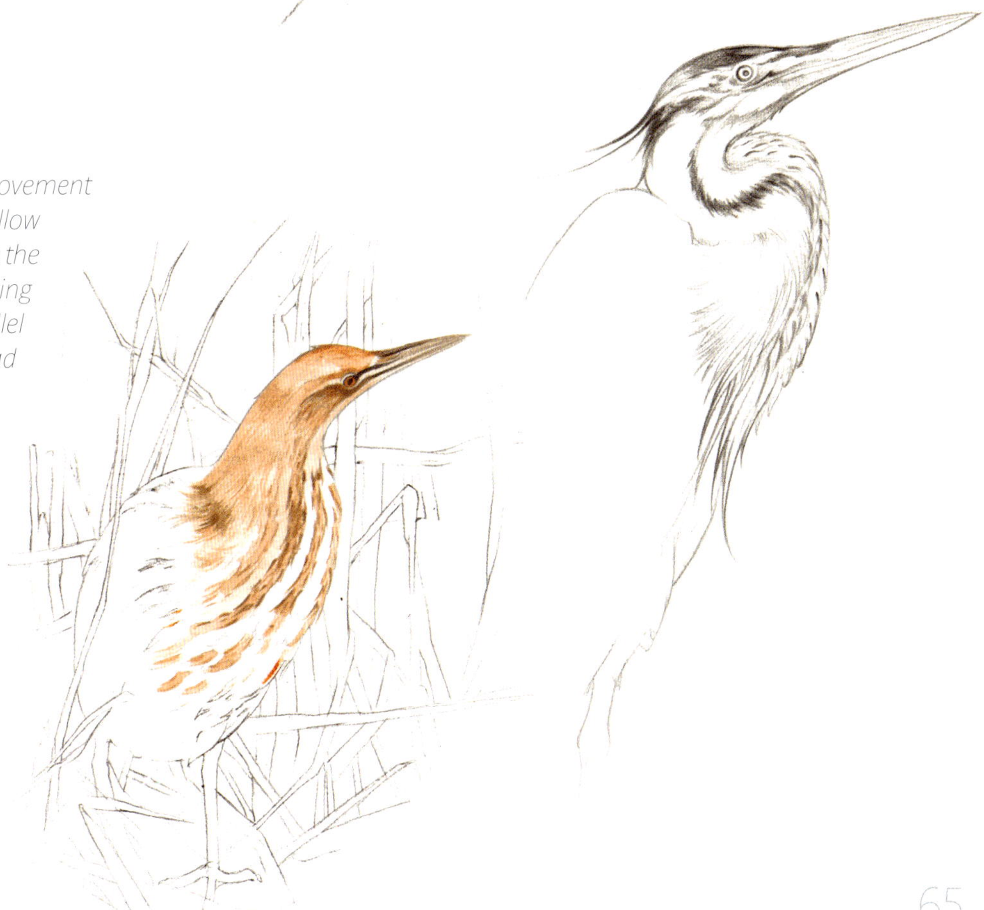

SMALL SANDERLING

Sanderlings trot lightly along the shore. Their pale, elegant plumage and their unusual style of movement make them fascinating models. A small study, such as this one, can be completed very quickly.

Colors:

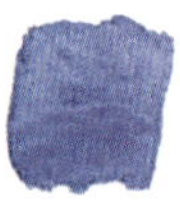

Cerulean Blue

Payne's Gray

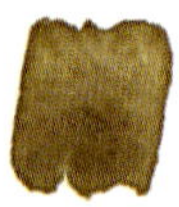

Raw Umber

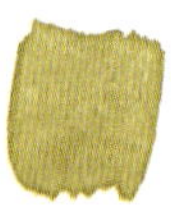

Burnt Umber

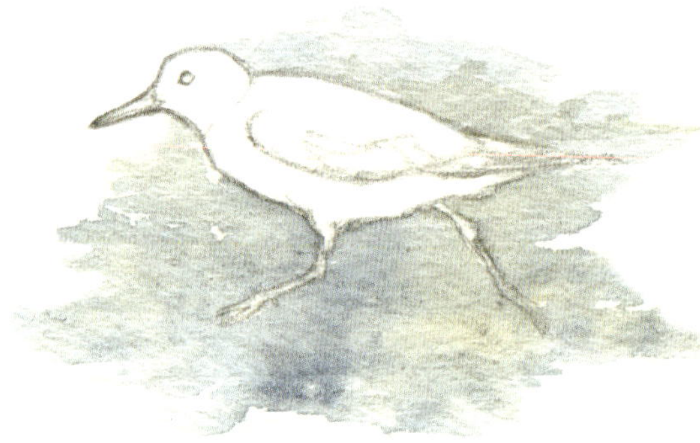

1. Make a rudimentary sketch of the bird. Moisten the background well, being careful when you go around the contours of the subject. Alternately apply a mixture of Cerulean Blue and Payne's Gray, and a dilution of Raw Umber. Let them overlap.

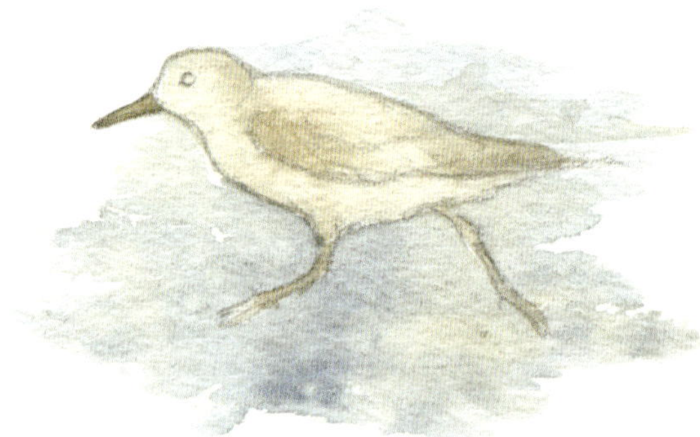

2. Apply washes of Burnt Umber and Raw Umber on the bird.

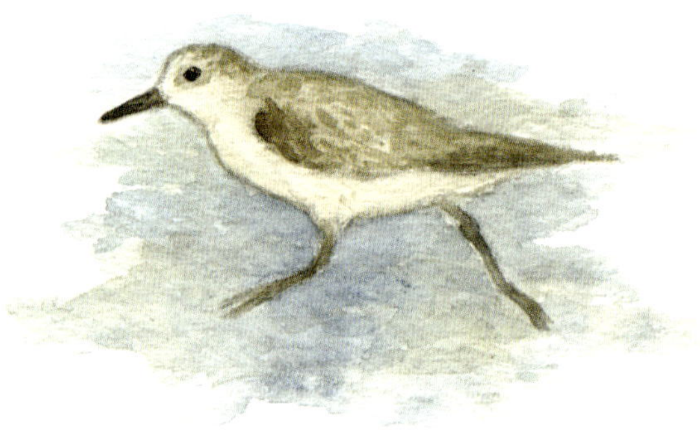

3. Progressively deepen the tones. The colored background is effective in highlighting the sanderling with its light plumage. Its faint contours and the horizontal brushstrokes give a sense of the bird's movement as well as that of the water.

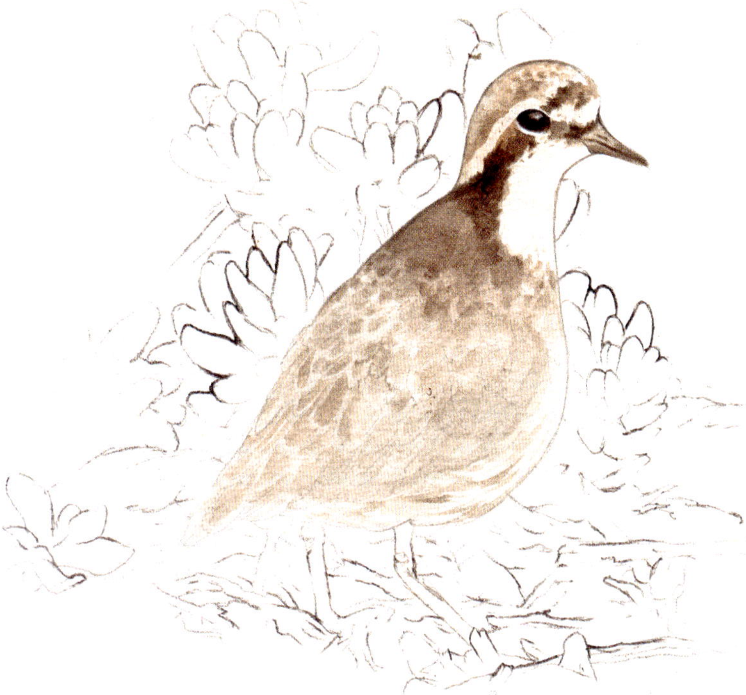

Bird Studies

The plumage of certain birds is ideally suited to working with a restricted range of colors.

With great efficiency, the birds here are shown in their natural habitat, which is implied through a few pencil strokes. Most of the image is left uncolored in order to give it lightness and vigor.

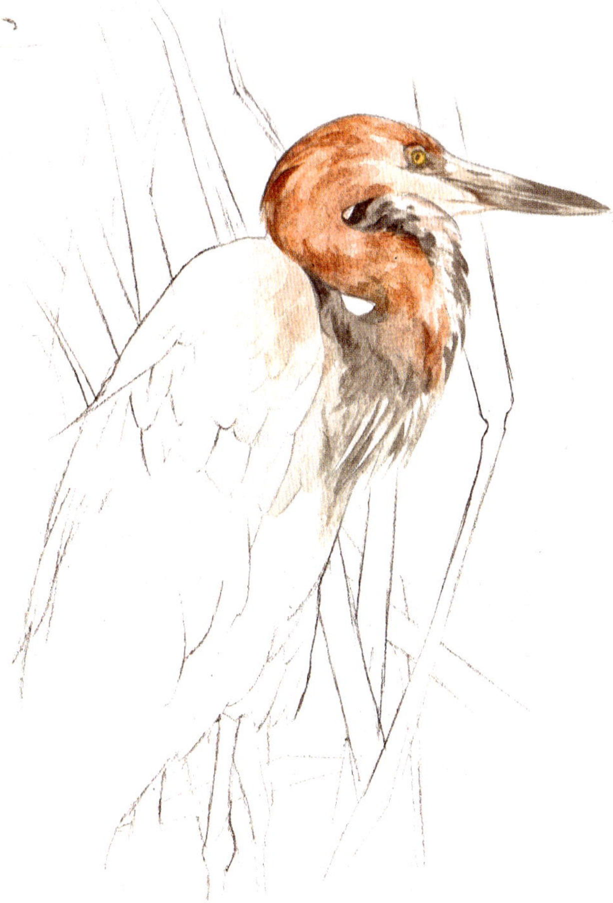

GREBES

These superb aquatic birds are often seen in ponds, marshes, and wet areas with dense vegetation. Make sure to come equipped with a good pair of binoculars and a folding chair.

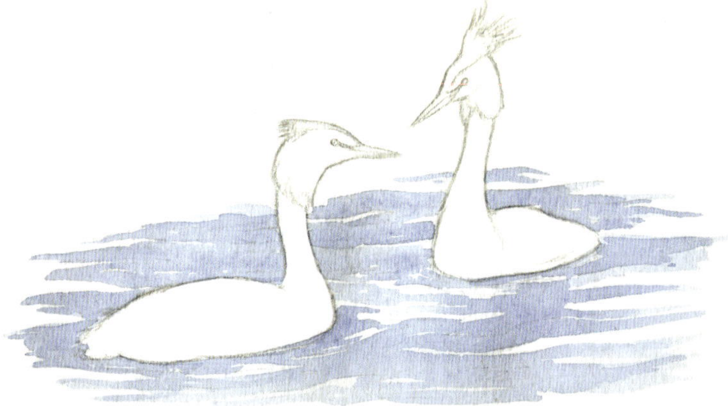

Colors:

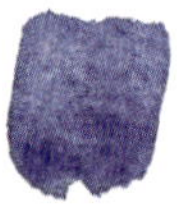
Ultramarine Blue

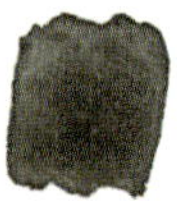
Payne's Gray

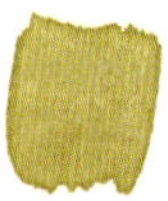
Raw Umber

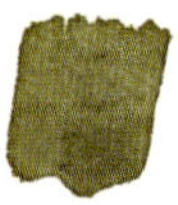
Sepia

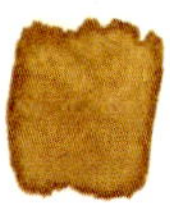
Burnt Sienna

1. Reserving the white of the paper for the birds, suggest ripples of water with soft brushstrokes, using a mixture of Ultramarine Blue and Payne's Gray.

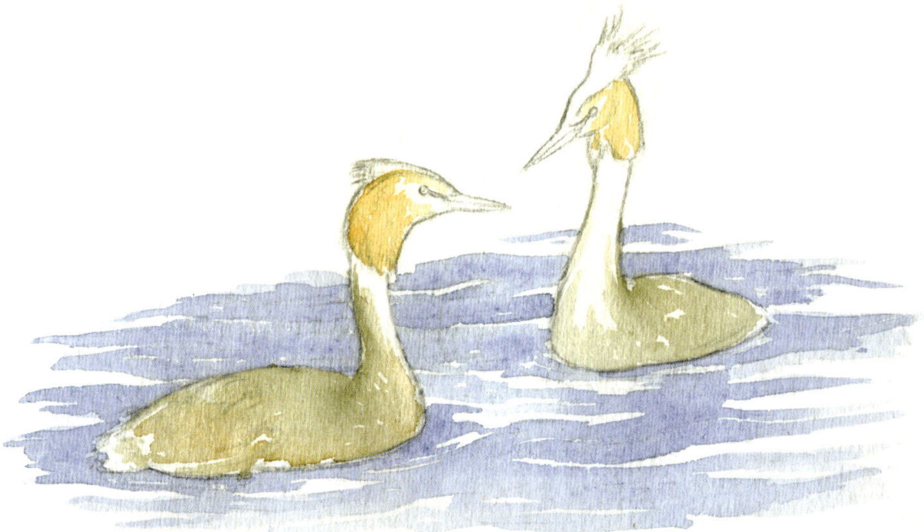

2. Apply a very light wash of Raw Umber, Sepia, and Payne's Gray on the bodies, and a mixture of Burnt Sienna and Raw Umber on the heads.

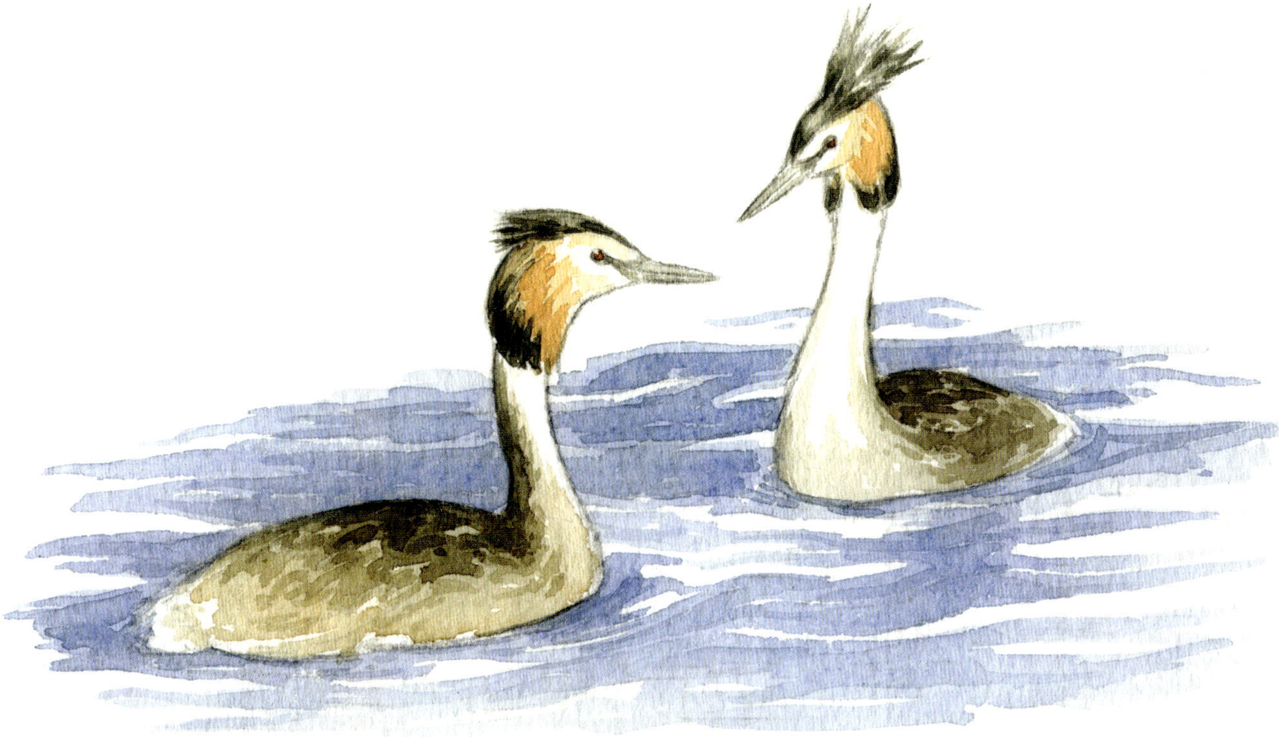

3. Apply a second wash to the blue water, darkening the areas surrounding the birds. Darken the backs and part of the necks of the birds (leaving their throats white) with small, sustained strokes of Sepia and Payne's Gray. Enliven the neck ruff with small outward strokes of Burnt Sienna. Using a fine brush, color the dark feathers with a wash of Payne's Gray.

HILLS AND SEA

This open landscape emphasizes the sky and sea. To create a misty sky, work in wet-on-wet! By allowing the colors to overlap and blend, you can represent the changing colors of the coast.

Colors:

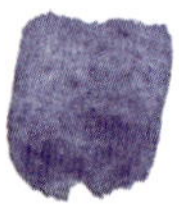 Ultramarine Blue

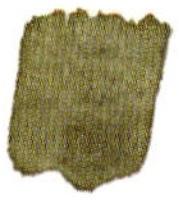 Sepia

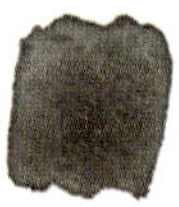 Payne's Gray

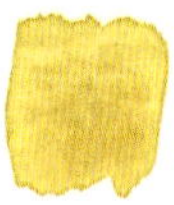 Yellow Ochre

 Rose Doré

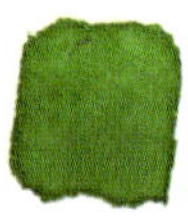 Hooker's Green

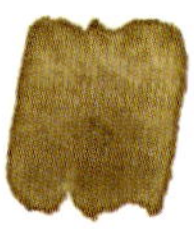 Burnt Umber

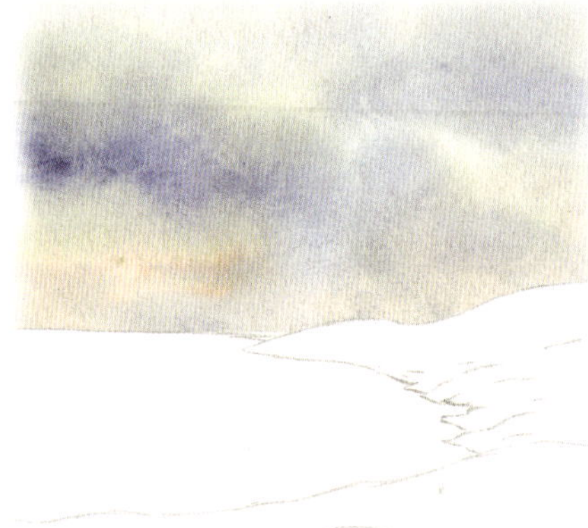

1. Fully moisten the entire section of sky. Apply a very diluted wash of Ultramarine Blue and Payne's Gray, then add a touch of Rose Doré, letting it flow in the moisture, mixing with other colors.

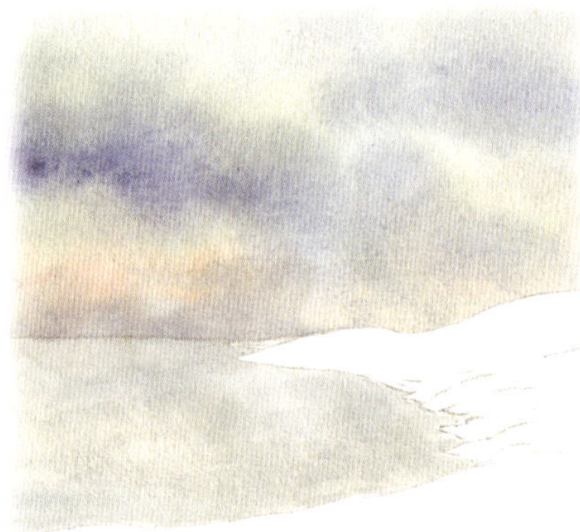

2. Moisten the section of sea, then apply a mixture of Payne's Gray and Ultramarine Blue. Gently darken the sky above the line of the horizon with a diluted mixture of Rose Doré and Ultramarine Blue.

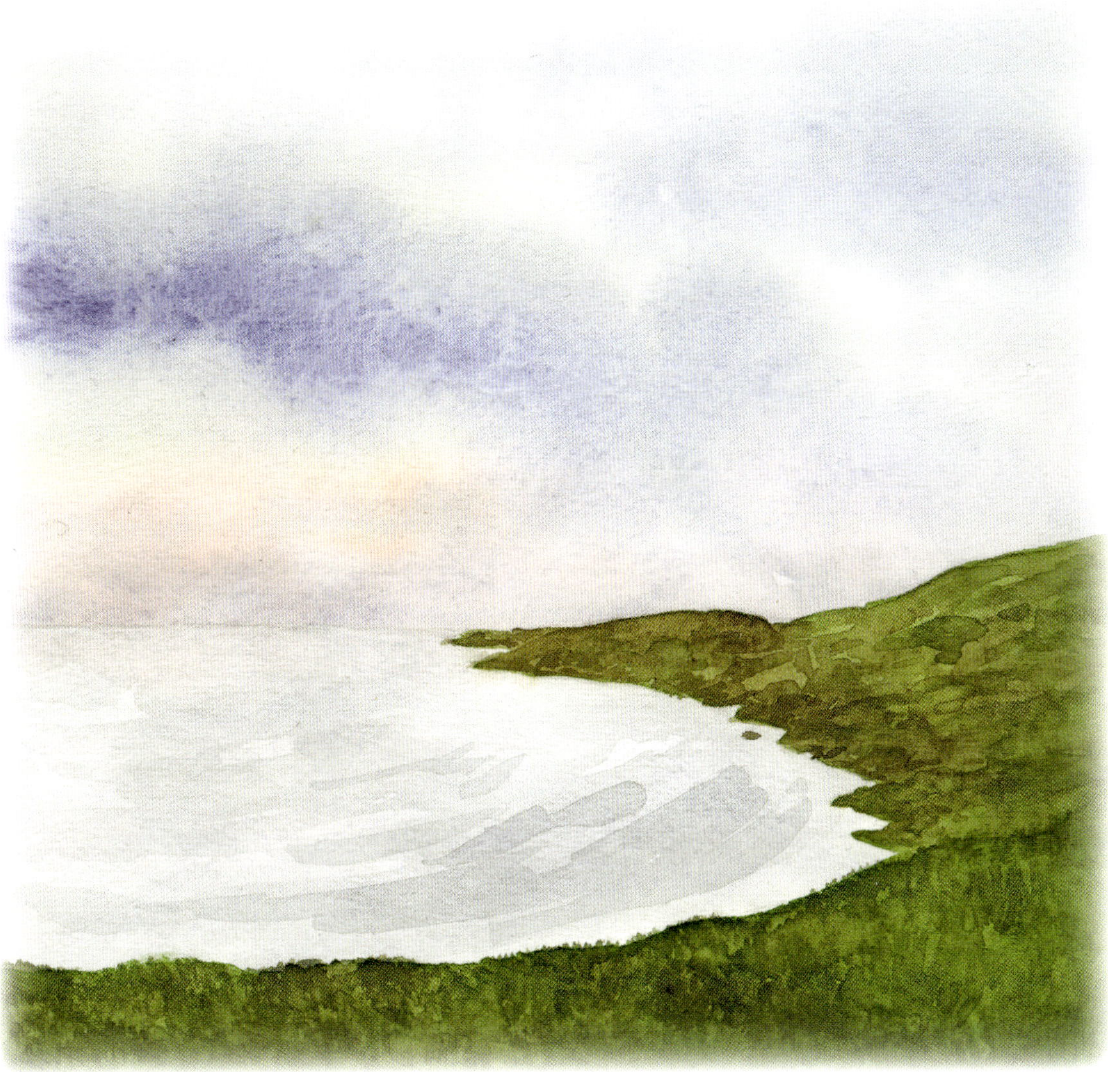

3. Moisten the grassy areas and apply a mixture of Hooker's Green, Burnt Umber, and Yellow Ochre. Add dimension to the coast with a mixture of Hooker's Green, Burnt Umber, and Sepia. Suggest tufts of grass in the foreground using small vertical brushstrokes of a mixture of Hooker's Green and Burnt Umber. Add some movement to the sea with a diluted mixture of Payne's Gray and Ultramarine Blue.

ICY MOUNTAIN

Water can also be ice and snow. This ambitious composition lets you play with leaving areas unpainted to make masterful use of the whiteness and luminosity of the paper.

Colors:

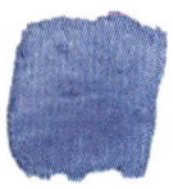
Cerulean Blue

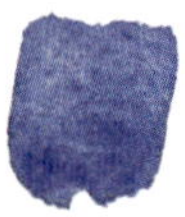
Ultramarine Blue

Payne's Gray

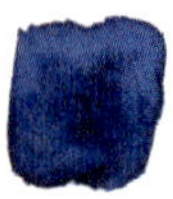
Prussian Blue

1. Sketch the mountains on regular paper first, then trace or transfer a cleaned-up version of your drawing onto a sheet of watercolor paper. It's best to work large for this piece. Moisten the reverse side of the paper with a sponge and attach the sheet to a flat board using gummed paper tape so that the watercolor paper doesn't buckle. After drying, apply a very light wash of Cerulean Blue on the entire sheet. Let it dry, then moisten the area of the sky and apply a mixture of Ultramarine Blue and Payne's Gray to it with uneven strokes. Remove excess paint with a wash brush.

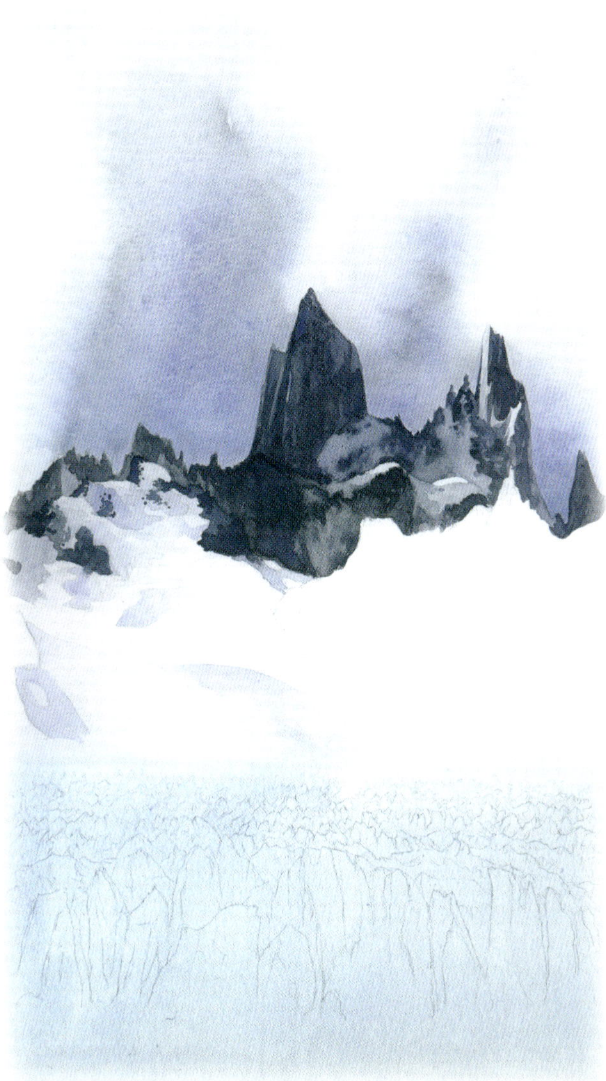

2. Next, apply a light wash of Ultramarine Blue and Payne's Gray on the upper mountains, then add details and dimension to them with a mixture of Prussian Blue, Payne's Gray, and Ultramarine Blue. Increase the proportion of Prussian Blue for the peaks and the most distant mountains. Give a sense of the snow's volume with a very diluted mixture of Ultramarine Blue and Payne's Gray.

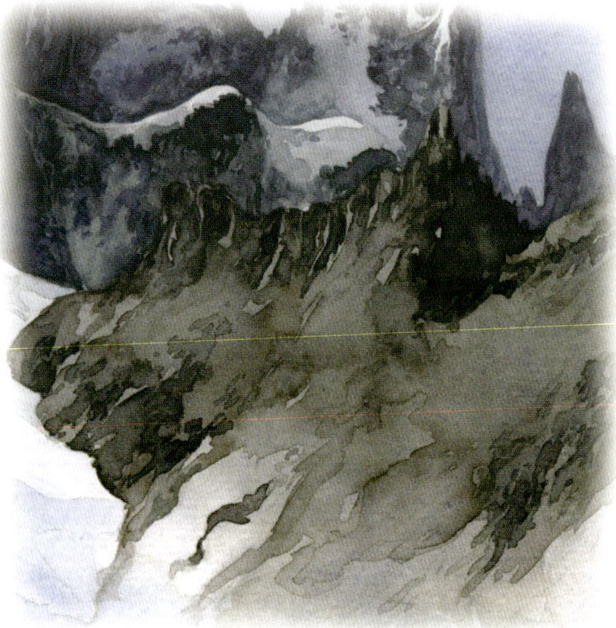

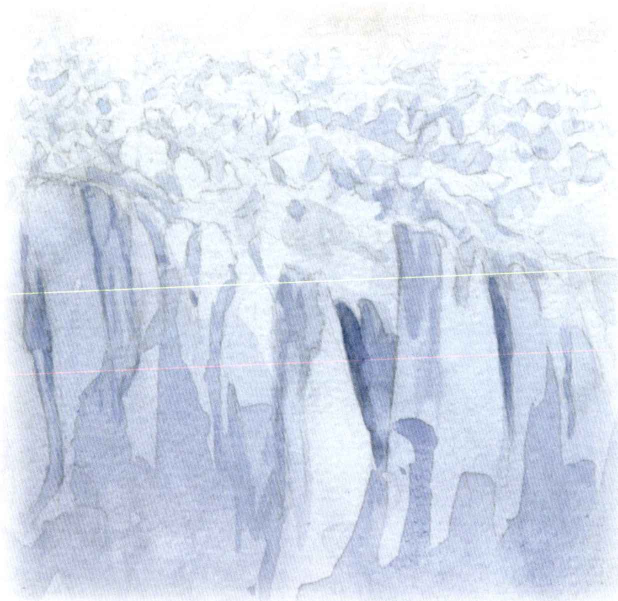

3. Moisten the chain of mountains on the right and apply a mixture of Payne's Gray with a drop of Prussian Blue to these mountains in a gradient. Emphasize several peaks and crags with a second, diluted wash of this same mixture. Finish by painting the ice formations in the foreground with a mixture of Cerulean Blue and Payne's Gray, diluting the mix for the more distant ice formations.

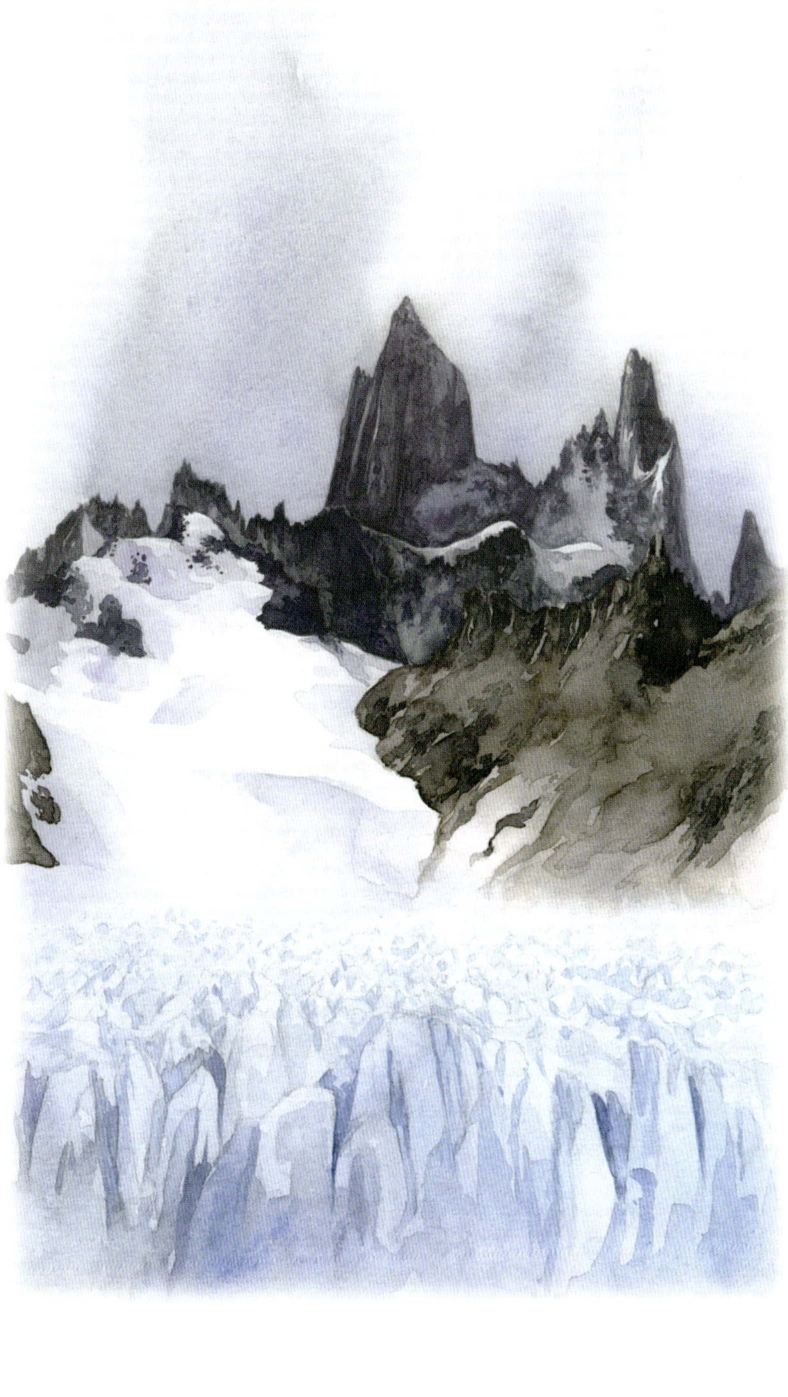

SNOWDROP

The snow has melted and here come the first snowdrops! These flowers offer a first delicate taste of the upcoming explosion of springtime color, and they help the artist to be patient, brush in hand.

Colors:

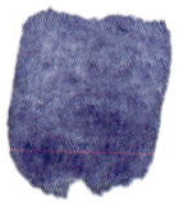
Cerulean Blue

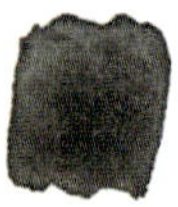
Payne's Gray

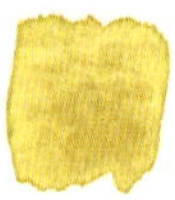
Yellow Ochre

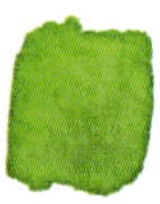
Sap Green

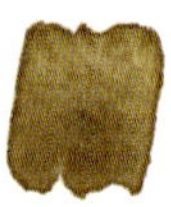
Burnt Umber

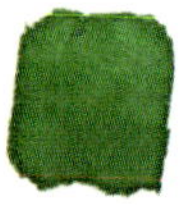
Hooker's Green

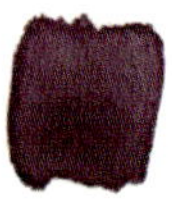
Permanent Mauve

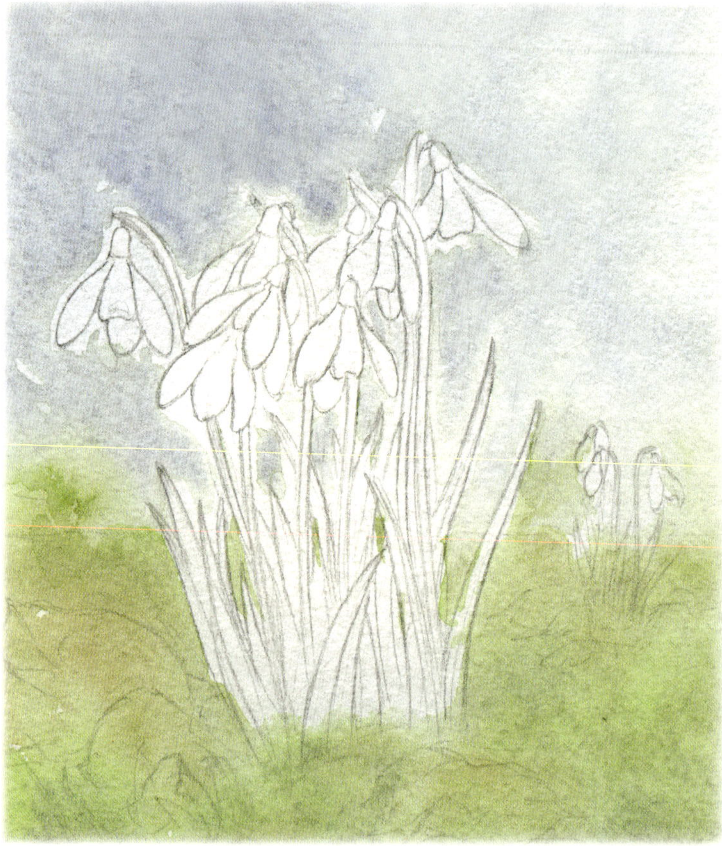

1. Moisten the background and apply a diluted wash of Ultramarine Blue and Payne's Gray to the sky. Then apply a mixture of Yellow Ochre, Sap Green, and Burnt Umber to the grass. Let the colors blend where they meet.

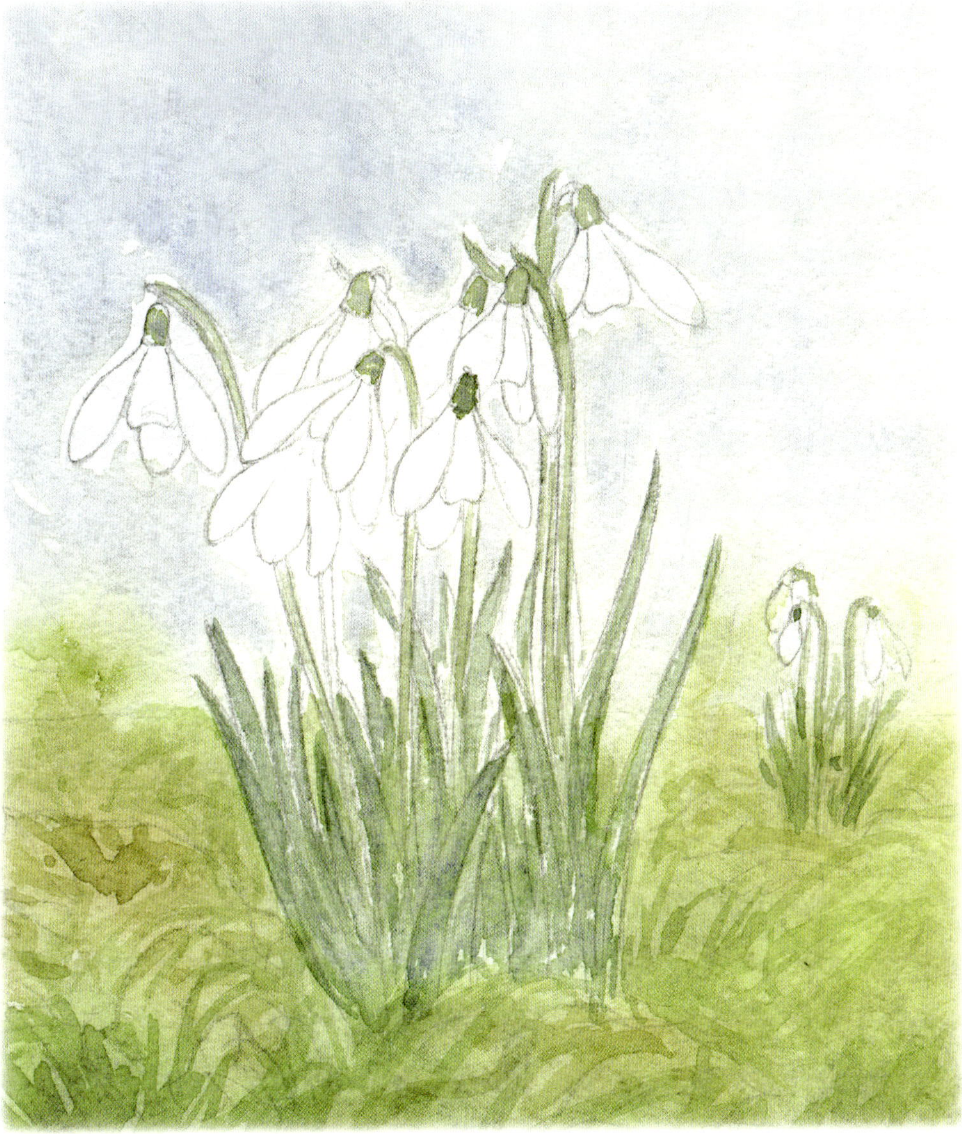

2. Paint the stems and the leaves with a mixture of Hooker's Green and Yellow Ochre. Then add a bit of body to the wet ground with the help of a second wash of Yellow Ochre, Sap Green, and Burnt Umber, applied with light strokes.

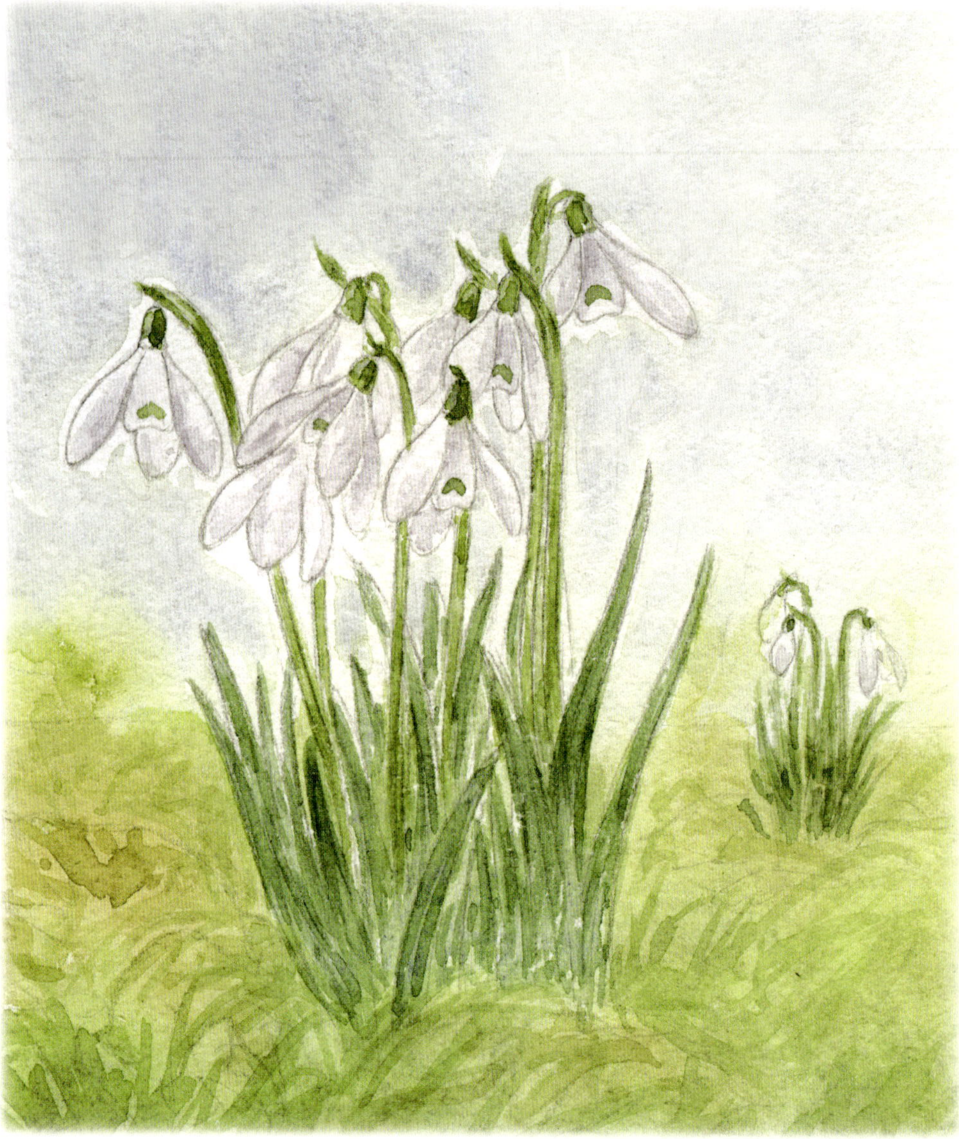

3. Apply a very light mixture of Mauve and Payne's Gray to the petals, making sure to leave a few luminous white areas. Then, apply a second wash of this same hue to reinforce their depth.

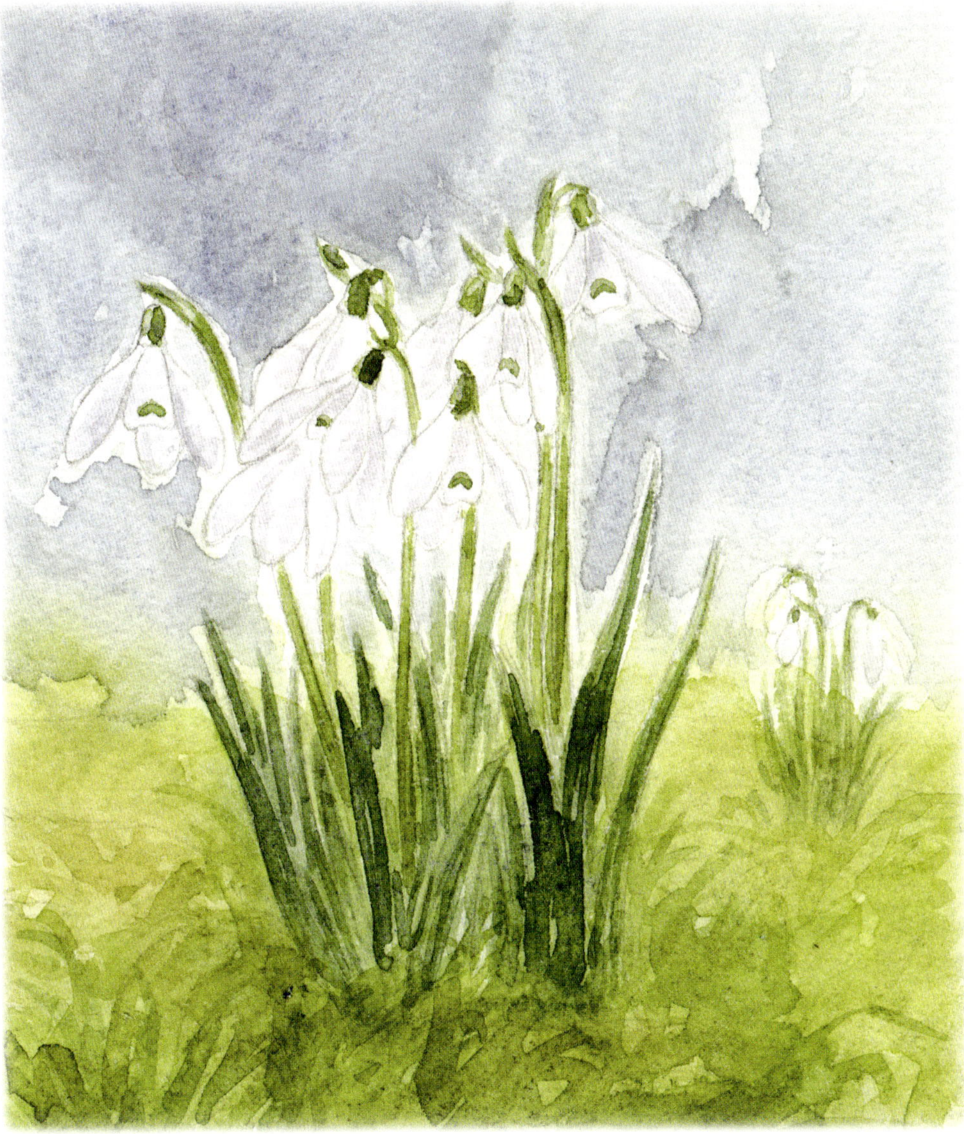

4. Moisten the sky, avoiding the flowers, and apply a fairly dark wash of Ultramarine Blue and Payne's Gray to it. Against this sky, the brightness of the snowdrops will stand out clearly. For the same purpose, darken the stems and leaves with a wash of Hooker's Green and Payne's Gray, then the ground with a wash of Sap Green and Yellow Ochre.

If you enjoyed this book, try other art titles from Peter Pauper Press, including:

Instructional Books

Calligraphy *by Jane Sullivan*
Colored Pencil Animal Kingdom *by Liu Xiaone*
Drawing for Everyone: Classic and Creative Fundamentals *by Bruce Waldman*

Interactive Art Books

The Çomics Journal *by Bruce Waldman*
The Daily Artist *by Marc Johns*
Hand-Lettering *by Megan Wells*
How to Draw Dragons *by Jane Sullivan*
Illuminated Letters *by Jane Sullivan*
Urban Sketchbook *by Gilles Ronin*
Zen Sketchbook *by Violette Bénlian*

Studio Series™ Art Supplies

Dry Gouache Paint Set
Aqua Brushes
Artist's Brush Set
Watercolor Crayons
Acrylic Paint Set
Colored Pencil Set and Deluxe Colored Pencil Set
25-Piece Drawing Set
Roll-Up Canvas Pencil Wrap
Professional Pencil Sharpener
Micro-Line Pen Set and Colored Micro-Line Pen Set
Fine-Line Marker Set
Dual-Tip Alcohol Markers
Premium Sketchbooks
Premium Drawing Pads
Artist's Tile Sets
Artist's Tile Postcards

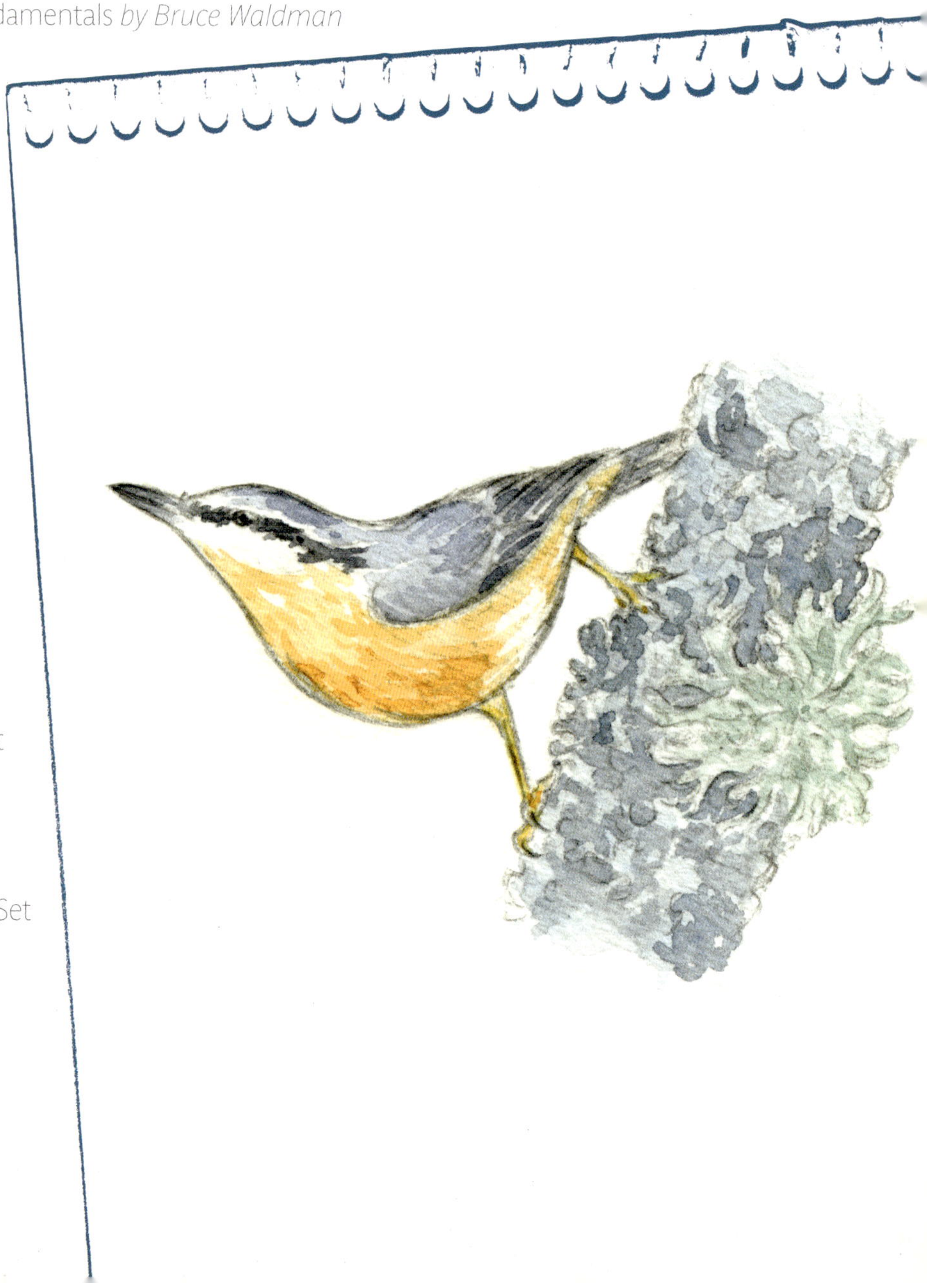